Click Me Baby
One More Time

How Your Relationship With Digital Media Has Shaped Your Life

Geo Ellen James

GW00750214

A CIP catalogue record for this book is available from the British Library.

ISBN 978-1-3999-9035-6

For my Bren.

For encouraging me to *write The Book,*
then reminding me to *write The Book,*
then telling me to *write The Book,*
then blocking out time in my calendar and taking our boys out
regularly in order to force me to *write The Book.*

Contents

Click Me Baby One More Time...

Foreword

I wrote this book with so much love and care, so that you can absolutely destroy it. There is nothing more lovely to me than a dog-eared, scribbled on, tea-stained book. I hope you fold down the pages to keep your place and circle the parts you wish to return to. I hope you pass this around to your friends, and your mum. I hope it ends up on the shelf of a community library in a package holiday hotel.

This book can be enjoyed in a linear fashion and I designed it to appeal in its entirety to all who read it, but I've also planned the chapters to be self-contained topics which you may wish to dive into separately.

Almost every word of this book was written during the early months of both of my boys' lives, over the course of two and a half years. The process was extremely cathartic for me during such a vulnerable and uncertain time, but also meant that thousands of words never made it into this final draft as they were incomprehensible ramblings of a passionate yet exhausted slug-woman.

There are sections of this book which may be quite difficult to read; I certainly found them difficult to write, but it's also filled with humour and joy and hope which reflects my general worldview. I

Click Me Baby One More Time…

do hope that people don't find this to be a gloomy read, but it was important to me that Click Me Baby One More Time was informative, factual and an accurate snapshot of the world in this current time. I hope it ages horribly.

Under the Influence

Under the Influence

Every day, the average person spends around eight hours engaging with screens—more time than they spend sleeping. This fact is even more pronounced for new parents, who often find themselves scrolling for comfort in the wee hours while feeding or rocking their baby. I wrote the majority of these chapters during those vulnerable first months with each of my boys. Watching them grow, I became increasingly fearful of the online world I'd been instrumental in building, a world they will soon be fully immersed in. This book is a deep dive into how those hours online are spent, what they're doing to our minds and culture, and how we can better understand the digital world that's become an integral part of our lives. I've spent the most recent part of my career teaching people how to protect themselves and their families from the dangers that the digital age poses whilst still empowering them to harness and adapt to the inevitable, ever-changing technological landscape. I think I do this largely in part to attempt to assuage a mounting guilt that I've been contributing for many years to some of the greatest problems of our lifetime.

In today's world, social media has become an inescapable presence, deeply woven into the fabric of our society. It has fundamentally altered the way we communicate, consume information, and engage with the world around us. With billions of users worldwide, spending an average of 145 minutes per day scrolling through feeds and engaging with content, the digital platforms we use every day have undeniably -and, many think somewhat tragically- become a central pillar of modern life. Navigating this new territory comes with more prominent and widely documented perils, such as sex crimes, data fraud and grooming, catfishing and hacking. But what about the less obvious and more insidious dangers of digital platforms? The burgeoning threat to our democratic system, the attack on our self-worth, or the equality recession? Amidst the endless scrolling and constant connection, how has social media reshaped our understanding of identity and togetherness? What are the long-term consequences of living in a digital ecosystem that thrives on likes, shares and validation? As our online lives become increasingly intertwined with our offline existence, how do we reconcile the digital and the real?

As we navigate the digital landscape, we find our virtual lives and real lives colliding in profound ways. The boundaries between online and offline existence blur, and the digital realm infiltrates our daily routines, relationships, and self-perception. A notification on our smartphones has the power to alter our mood, while a viral post can shape our worldview. We curate our online personas, carefully selecting the moments and aspects of our lives to share, often grappling with the dichotomy between authenticity and aspiration. Our online interactions can lead to real-world consequences, from building connections and mobilising for social change to experiencing cyberbullying or falling victim to online scams. Through social media, we can change our careers, find our next husband and learn how to make cheese. We can choose where to eat on holiday, buy a lumbar support cushion, tell anyone who will listen how much it's changed our lives, and then sell it after discovering it three years later under the spare bed.

-

In the early days of social media, platforms like Myspace and blogs revolutionised online communication and self-expression. These spaces offered individuals unprecedented freedom to share their thoughts, creativity, and personal stories. At age 11, I created an "e-zine" on a web-hosting site that combined my passion for rescue donkeys, The Simpsons and Gareth Gates. It included a list of animal shelters and their phone numbers for making donations, a rudimentary interactive quiz to find out whether you were "more of a Bart or a Lisa", and a Gareth page, a screenshot of which - upon reflection- could be used as evidence against me in court for any number of crimes (the page in question contained sections of The Unfortunate Mr Gates' features -his tooth gap, his hair gel spikes, his freckles- roughly cut out on Microsoft Paint and left floating in a nightmarish rankings list of 'cutest' to 'least cutest').

In this newness, suddenly, people could connect with like-minded individuals from around the world, creating virtual communities centred around shared interests and passions. It was a pivotal moment that challenged the traditional media gatekeepers and paved the way for democratised content creation. As social media evolved, platforms such as Facebook and Instagram gained prominence, forever altering the landscape of personal connections and social interactions. The rise of these platforms coincided with a shift in how we perceive and present ourselves to others. The pressure to curate a polished online presence and accumulate social validation through likes and comments became prevalent. I've been connected professionally to the social media industry for 15 years - since long before it became an industry. Throughout this time, I've worked with some of the biggest names online. I've represented women with a following of millions, walked red carpets with people who "post selfies" for a living, countersigned seven-figure contracts, and sweated through PR crises. I've sat in editing suites as people were picked apart for their *imperfections* – a spot on their chin, an unsightly armpit, or, heaven forbid, a stray hair! I've watched from the front row as women criticise and are criticised in an evergreen public forum.

Shockingly, I never made it to the Big Time with donkeysandsimpsonsaresocool.com, but millions of people with their own corners of the internet have. These individuals -many call them "Influencers"- have harnessed the power of social media platforms to build personal brands, amass large followings, and monetise their opinions on brands and products. Throughout my career, I've watched many digital content creators, some of them close friends, raised up and torn down by fans, the press, brands and each other. I have observed and been a part of the evolution of influencer culture and its impact on consumer behaviour. Like it or not, creators impact most peoples' lives today, whether through the content they consume on their devices or the purchasing decisions they make. Social media's influence extends beyond personal lives. It has become a powerful tool for shaping the zeitgeist, influencing politics and social change, and impacting the economy.

-

My beginnings were humble. I was raised by a single mother who was raised by a single mother, and we lived in rented accommodations in small, quiet towns for the majority of my upbringing. Entering the world of corporate beauty PR felt like stepping onto the set of the Devil Wears Prada on acid, and I've always been unavoidably aware of how not at home I feel in the industry that has been my constant for my entire adult life. The industry which preaches body positivity whilst perpetuating unattainable beauty standards. Where brands compete to deliver the most *diverse* campaigns but whose workforce is in the overwhelming majority white, middle class and not disabled. In the past decade, the authenticity and transparency of influencer marketing have come under scrutiny. As we explore the rise of influencers, we must delve into the ethical implications of the 'Creator Economy' and the roles that those who exist in and earn money from it play in everyone's lives. What responsibilities do social media creators and marketers carry as culture leaders? With most of the world online, the power to amplify voices, spark movements, and challenge established norms lies at the fingertips of every individual with an internet connection. Does this then mean that the accountability sits with all of us?

Under the Influence

Social media has been a more significant part of my life than it is for the billions of people worldwide who scroll daily. I use these chapters to share statistics, anecdotes and insights I've collected over a decade of my love/hate relationship with the online world, woven in with the historical levers and drivers that have led us to this point. I like to acknowledge all facets of this space, however. Whilst there are clear connections between Instagram and low self-esteem, Twitter and cancel culture, digital journalism and rampant sexism, there are also great victories for progress, particularly intersectional progress, which have emerged through the democratising power of digital voice.

Desperate Housewives

Desperate Housewives

One of the most significant impacts of social media lies in its influence on the evolution of gender roles and the portrayal of gender in popular culture. Through platforms like Instagram, TikTok, and YouTube, individuals have gained unprecedented control over their personal narratives and self-presentation. Social change in recent years has laid the foundations for independence and freedom of choice for previously marginalised groups, and notably for women and their roles within the home. But can a woman's choice to stay at home in the 2020s be considered a feminist act - a reclamation of independence? Or does it perpetuate a cycle that normalises female homemaking as the ideal gender split? Can there be such a thing as a free will choice when we are so heavily influenced by bias and other external factors drip-fed to us through our screens on an hourly basis?

Throughout the chapters of human existence, gender roles, particularly in traditional household dynamics, have been shaped and reshaped in line with numerous factors such as religious pressures and technological advancements. During various periods, women have fought to break free from the confines of the "homemaker" label, striving for autonomy, empowerment, and the opportunity to chart their own paths. Yet, as we navigate the complexities of the modern age with its newfound levels of choice and relative gender equality, we find ourselves confronting a paradox—a resurgence of classic gender dynamics that can be both empowering and potentially harmful.

Click Me Baby One More Time…

History often tells us that men have contributed to the development of the world more than women have. Patriarchy cherry picks for its history books, silencing women and their roles in innovation, discovery and progress. Give yourself 10 seconds right now to name as many self-made billionaires as you can. I wouldn't blame you if your list mainly consisted of old white men, not least because currently the majority of the world's billionaires are old white men (just 5 per cent of the world's wealthiest people are self-made women), but also because society and media tend to take a far greater interest in the Elons and Marks vs the Judy Faulkners and Folorunso Alakijas. In fact, the first self-made American millionaire was a Black woman. Her name was Madam Walker, and she made her money by creating and selling cosmetics and hair care products for Black women.

Similarly, when we look back at prehistory, we typically imagine that cavemen were *the* hunter-gatherers and that women would have simply withered away without them. The truth is that during this period, women gathered between 75 per cent and 80 per cent of the food stocks. They also invented many tools and discovered the healing properties of certain plants and herbs (which technically made them some of the first doctors). However, even though our Stone Age sisters were doing the sabretooth's share of hunting and gathering, Neolithic men make up the majority of discovered formal burials and are placed front and centre in cave paintings.

The Hebrew Bible suggests that the ideal woman "considers a field and buys it; out of her earnings, she plants a vineyard". In this same era, ancient Egyptian, Persian, Grecian and Roman women (in wealthier families) were tasked with managing enslaved people and staff and, in some scenarios, were even permitted to work towards becoming priestesses. We know that the ancient Egyptians had some female deities, and we believe that around 4% of all pharaohs were women. Midwifery, hairdressing and perfumery were also *acceptable* roles for women. However, it was still unheard of for women of this time to be educated or literate, and marriage was primarily a transaction between patriarchs.

In the Middle Ages, women continued to be auxiliary to their husbands and fathers, sometimes leaving their domestic duties to support in the fields and factories during busy periods. Interestingly, whilst married mediaeval women were legally dependent on their husbands, their unmarried counterparts could sign contracts, borrow money and run their own businesses. If a businesswoman married, her assets were independently protected by law, meaning that even if her husband filed for bankruptcy, she did not owe his creditors. The British Museum recently held an exhibition of some cool examples of female business cards from the 16th-18th century, with fanmakers, milliners and pharmacists offering their wares in London's Cheapside. In some areas of Western Europe, women were thought to be more literate than men as the latter were often pushed toward a life of combat.

Despite the almost 64-year reign of a female monarch during this period, the 19th-century "understanding" of gender was that women were morally superior yet physically inferior to men, leaving them much better suited to a role within the home. In poorer families where multiple incomes were necessary, women were permitted to work only in jobs where children also made up a large proportion of the workforce, such as in textile factories. Damn, these nimble fingers! In middle and higher-class homes, the Victorians took a stringent view of what made an "accomplished" woman (read: a woman who is able to attract and keep a good husband). Caroline Bingley in Jane Austin's Pride and Prejudice lists these desirable traits as "a thorough knowledge of music, singing, drawing, dancing, and the modern languages …; and besides all this, she must possess a certain something in her air and manner of walking, the tone of her voice, her address and expressions …". I'm exhausted just thinking about it, although if becoming a one-woman show will catch me a Mr Darcey (I'm a Colin Firth gal), then maybe it's worth it.

Click Me Baby One More Time…

It's a common misconception that sex was entirely taboo at this time, with the pop culture of the time often skirting the subject with increasingly obscure innuendo. As Claire Jarvis writes in Exquisite Masochism: Marriage, Sex, and the Novel Form, "If you are reading a novel and all of a sudden the description becomes extremely 'thick,' you may be in the middle of an erotic scene." However, the reality is that sex was very much a topic of interest for Victorians, and it played a massive part in the gender disparity of the time. The pinnacle of social acceptance for 19th-century women was the "Angel in the House" archetype - inaugurated in Coventry Patmore's famous poem of the same name, describing a devoted and submissive housewife whose piety and chastity made her the model for all women to aspire to. Women were expected to remain innocent and chaste even in marriage (and motherhood!?). The antithesis of The Angel was "the fallen woman", a broad term found across Victorian literature and legislation to describe any women who partook in extra-marital relations. Laws at the time also reflected this hypocritical mindset, with STD epidemics being blamed almost entirely on female sex workers (not the often married men who were paying for their services) and divorce being enforceable against women for a single act of adultery versus men who were permitted additional offences before a divorce would be considered.

One of the catalysts for women's liberation was World War I. Many men had to go to war, leaving women to take on typically male roles and positions. The women's suffrage movement had long been fighting for equal rights and the right to vote, and while the war effort seemed to disrupt their progress somewhat, it was also demonstrative that women were, as it happened, capable of contributing to the economic status of a "modern" country. During the Second World War, media like radio and posters significantly pushed women towards traditionally male-dominated labour. The American "Rosie the Riveter" poster epitomised this message. Created in 1942, it featured a determined woman flexing her arm with the slogan "We Can Do It!" above. It aimed to inspire women

14

to join the workforce and support the war effort and is still often used in pop culture and as a fancy dress muse, still symbolising empowerment for many. But did women genuinely have a choice, or were they driven by necessity and social pressure? With Rosie glaring down at them in the bread aisle during the air raids, was there anything else to do besides roll sleeves and don workboots? Economic factors and societal expectations pressured them to fill roles left vacant by men. Though they challenged gender norms temporarily, the pressure to return to traditional roles resurfaced after the war. Unequal treatment, lower wages, and limited opportunities endured.

After years of protesting, women (but only the white ones) gained the right to vote in the UK and the United States by 1920. This marked a significant milestone in women's suffrage, granting them an active role in society beyond the confines of wives and caretakers. Following the war, more women entered the workforce, working in factories and earning their own wages. They experienced a process of emancipation and enjoyed newfound financial independence. However, the tumultuous events of the 20th century, including two World Wars, the Great Depression, large-scale immigration and urbanisation, and technological advancements, created a desire for stability and structure, and, as the typical Western family had more wealth than previous generations, this meant that the family could be divided into the roles of caretaker and breadwinner. Fifty points, if you can guess the most common gender split here.

As a collective subconscious drive to recover from shared trauma, Western culture looked to nostalgia as a remedy - a notion I feel may be close to home for readers in the 2020s. A pre-war society appealed, with a man heading up the household and his faithful woman bringing up the rear (and rearing up the kids). This lifestyle was upheld and perpetuated by the pop culture and advertising industries. Despite not appointing their first female editor-in-chief until 1994, Good Housekeeping was biblical to the average mid-century American woman, with a subscriber base of nearly half of all women between the ages of 18 and 49. The magazine's objective was "to produce and perpetuate perfection as may be obtained in the household", a task they succeeded in not unlikely because of the introduction of their "seal of approval", which recommended homemaking products and gadgets to their readership. A man's role was to earn money, and a woman's role was to spend that money on things that upheld the 1950s and '60s values of competitiveness, sightliness and societal conformity.

This longing for family and structure was fueled by media and marketing, which popularised the idea of the nuclear family (mom+pop+kids) as part of the American Dream, which trickled down throughout Europe and other colonised countries. During this era, popular culture played a pivotal role in influencing and reinforcing the idea of the nuclear family. Television shows like "The Jetsons" portrayed an idealised futuristic family, with the desirable family structure consisting of a father, a mother, and two children. It painted a picture of a perfect family unit living in a world where technology served to simplify their lives and strengthen family bonds.

Additionally, "The Dick Van Dyke Show" provided another example of how pop culture reinforced the nuclear family ideal. This popular American sitcom, which aired in the 1960s, showcased the lives of Rob and Laura Petrie, a married couple with one son. The show portrayed Rob as the breadwinner and showcased Laura's role as a supportive wife and mother. It presented an image of the nuclear family as a harmonious and loving unit, where the challenges and joys of family life were explored with humour and relatability.

These examples from pop culture demonstrate how media representations of the nuclear family influenced and reinforced societal expectations. By presenting idealised versions of family life, these shows contributed to the normalisation of traditional gender roles and family structures. They portrayed women as homemakers and nurturers, while men were depicted as providers and protectors. These portrayals, along with other media influences, played a role in shaping societal ideals and expectations regarding family life during that era. These references in pop culture had a tremendous impact on women's aspirations and choices. While some women may have found fulfilment in the roles depicted, others may have felt limited by the narrow definitions of gender roles and family dynamics presented in these shows.

It's commonplace nowadays to romanticise this era. Yes, the lads wore nice suits, and West Elm has made a killing on selling us the classic mid-century aesthetic (that'll be £2,000 for an armoire, thank you very much). Still, there's nothing glamorous about the rampant sexism, violent public racism and a general lack of human rights for anyone other than middle-class, non-disabled, cis, straight white men. In 1870, the New England Medical Gazette published a public warning that any woman who "sets out for a sea voyage or journey by rail" was at risk of "uterine dislocation". Nearly a whole century later, in 1967, Kathrine Switzer became the first woman to officially sign up for the Boston Marathon (not telling race officials she was female). She recalls in her memoir her male coach exclaiming, "No woman can run the Boston Marathon", arguing that a woman's body is too "fragile" to run such a distance. The director of the Boston Marathon was outraged and was quoted in the New York Times: "If that girl were my daughter, I'd spank her". To further add injury to insult, race manager Jock Semple repeatedly assaulted Katherine throughout the race, attempting to rip her race number from her clothing as she ran! She caused such a stir that the Amateure Athletic Union (AAU) banned all women from competing in "male" races. They finally backed down five years later, opening up the marathon to both men and women. So, in that hundred years, we may have gained permission to safely travel without the danger of throwing our female organs about the place, but we were still fighting to prove that our bodies were just as capable and worthy as men's.

Click Me Baby One More Time…

—

Before the digital revolution began, marketing for household appliances focussed on their efficacy and proximity to mid-century family values. In 1950s Australia, ads for Hoover's washing machines stated they simply "wash cleaner", whilst magazine marketing for Hills Hoist drying racks featured a housewife stating, "best present I could ask for! - I'll appreciate [the drying rack] for the rest of my life!". Wouldn't we all, Caroline? British ads for vacuum cleaners in the same era heroed phrases such as "you'll be happier with a Hoover", "she knows it's the best", and "world's finest cleaner". However, the effects of mass production and the innovation of the late 60s and 70s brought automation into middle-class homes, and this, tied with women's increased dissatisfaction with a life locked indoors, catalysed a societal shift. Betty Friedan sold 1 million copies of her 1963 book The Feminine Mystique, challenging the role women were being made to play within their families and bringing to light the results of her research, which proved how unfulfilling housework and child-rearing were for many women. As women started to reject traditional values, we saw a change of tone in advertising, with appliances beginning to upsell on their efficiency and time-saving properties. In this era, slogans such as "fully automatic", "totally simple", and "easy to use" mark the death of the forced-to-be-proud housewife and the rise of leisure time and liberation.

In 1968, the female workforce of Ford's factory in Dagenham, England, went on strike. They discovered that whilst male employees were pay-graded based on their skill level, experience, and hierarchy, there was a separate (and, on the whole, lower) pay grade specifically for women. Barbera Castle, the then Minister of Employment, was outraged for them, and this marked the beginning of the 1970 Equal Pay Act (which, at the time of writing, over 50 years later, has not yet resulted in true equality, but it certainly made a start!). Across Europe, America, and Australia, women started protesting for their reproductive rights, employment rights, and general equality. Because the cause for gender parity was so closely aligned with civil rights, this second wave of feminism significantly impacted modern-day philosophies. They protested gender roles, gender-based violence, and the objectification of women in society (issues that are still problematic in the 21st century). Women were becoming more in touch with their sexuality and sexual freedom, and this movement even laid the groundwork for gay rights and the LGBTQIA+ community.

Whilst the Woodstock era is synonymous with hippie culture, "free love," and the sexy sidekicks of Sean Connery's Bond, sexual empowerment was considered a radical concept for women to entertain. In 1964, Gerri Santoro, like many women before and since, died aged 28 whilst attempting an illegal abortion in fear of her abusive husband. The heart-wrenching police photo of her dead body became a symbol of the reproductive rights movement, sparking demonstrations across the Western world as women fought for easy and safe access to contraception and abortion. Despite Alfred Kinsley's successful sex survey in the 1940s (proving that women did, in fact, orgasm - who knew?), it wasn't until the 60's that science started investing in female orgasms, and it was discovered that some women could experience multiple orgasms and that orgasms could be achieved with vaginal or clitoral stimulation. Raise a glass to your ancestral sisters and their shit sex lives.

Pre-Victorian marriages typically involved an adult man and a female child aged between 12-14; by the 19th century, the average age of a bride was 20, and by 1997, this had reached 25, reflecting our exercising of personal choice in the matter of our own marriages. In the 90s, we saw a rise in strong female icons from Buffy to Lisa Simpson, Ashley Banks to the Spice Girls. We saw a surge in feminist organisations such as Riot Grrrl and an increase in female leaders such as the first American female Secretary of State (Madeleine Korbel Albright), the first female president of an Ivy League institution (Judith Rodin) and the first woman attorney general (Janet Reno). We also saw Britain's first female Prime Minister, but more on her later.

By the 90s, with increased access to education, employment opportunities, and reproductive rights, women embarked on a journey towards self-determination, challenging the notion that a woman's primary role was *homemaker*. Yet, a single generation later, in this era of unprecedented choice and autonomy, we find ourselves at a crossroads—a place where some women, through their own genuine desire or influenced by sociopolitical factors, are opting to embrace the role of the homemaker once more.

In 2008, I was 15 years old, looking like the "before" version of Mia Thermopolis. My book-one-Hermione hair, eyebrows, freckles, teeth too big for my face, and body type caught somewhere between Tammy Girl and Burton left me with about as much teenage sex appeal as Hubba Bubba caught in a wire retainer. I wasn't in the kind of Disney Channel girl gangs where we stayed up all night talking about our future husbands and what we wanted to name our kids. In fact, the Sims2 household I played as was myself all grown up and working in the city, dressing exactly the same as I did in my teens (complete with 8-ball-chain slung around the hips of my cargo pants) and living with my childhood cat. I have always wanted a family of my own, but - and this may be the result of growing up in a single-sex household- I'd always assumed that my aspirations and career goals would be front and centre, and should a man who looks suspiciously like my teen crush Ricky Wilson and some babies drop into my lap, I'd just crack on enjoying all of the above with minimal disruption.

GCSE German was one of my favourite subjects in school, and I'd not spent much time worrying about the exam, which had been sure to be an easy grade for me. Listening and Reading papers behind me, it was time to open the "writing" assignment, where we'd have an hour to answer a single question in an essay style. The question stopped me in my tracks. "Kariere Oder Familie?". *Career or family? Please write an engaging piece on which of these you would choose and why.*

The decision to prioritise family life over a career is often a deeply personal one, reflecting individual values, aspirations, and circumstances. But it also raises profound questions about the nature of choice, agency, and the complex interplay between societal norms and personal freedom. If a woman stays at home with her kids all day in lieu of working, is it because she wants to, because she thinks she wants to, or because society is set up in a way that leaves her no choice?

-

Since this revolution, and throughout the past few decades of what I'd call the toxic girl boss movement, the role of the unemployed woman was not only rejected but actively discriminated against. In 2012, Forbes magazine published an article with the headline "Are Housewives To Blame For The Plight Of Working Women?" addressing a whitepaper that revealed that men whose wives don't work "deny, more frequently, qualified female employees opportunities for promotions." Margaret Thatcher stated that single mothers should be denied child benefits and sent to a nunnery. No, really. 'The motherhood penalty' is a term used to describe the impact of bias against mums, usually in a professional capacity. With research showing that employers are 2.1 times more likely to give a callback to a woman who was not a parent than to an equally qualified mother, teamed with the rising cost of childcare often cancelling out any subsequent wages earned and a lack of flexibility by employers, it's no wonder that even despite an intention to work, many housewives remain just that.

My second maternity leave began two weeks after the end of a 12-month fixed-term contract. Some would say *great timing*, although those people wouldn't likely be in the position of dropping from a decent salary to government statutory pay during a cost of living crisis. Nor need to job hunt whilst breastfeeding, wiping bums, and accidentally answering the door to the food shop delivery man with their left nipple hanging out (it happened twice).

Maternity leave is <u>Hard. Core.</u> I've negotiated million-pound contracts, been responsible for the welfare of household name celebrities, run the backstage whirlwind for Naomi Campbell's show and organised global TV shoots. And the two periods of my life where I was nothing but Mum, all day, every day, were significantly more demanding, more stressful and yes, more rewarding than any job I've had. I'm fortunate enough that I have the choice. I can choose to be at home 24/7 with my kids, and I can also choose to spend 32 hours a week doing a job I love whilst earning money and the rest of my time with my family. Many of my friends and one million women in the UK do not work at all because of their caring responsibilities, and a considerable chunk of those are in a position where they'd love to be working, but the cost of the childcare needed to cover their shifts is more than the amount they'd earn, making going to work a financial burden on their family.

As with any marginalised group in the 21st century, women at home took to social media to find solidarity and comfort in a virtual community. In 2018, Essex housewife Sophie created an Instagram account for her first marital home where she shared her daily cleaning tips and routines. Just three months after launching her account, Mrs Hinch had one million followers, a fanbase self-titled the Hinch Army, and Sophie's favourite cleaning products were sold out all over the UK, with £1 sponges being listed at 30x their RRP on Amazon and eBay. Small family cleaning brand Zoflora needed to double its production and increased its sales by 28%, and Mrs Hinch's first (and then her fourth!) book made her a Sunday Times bestseller. But "The Hinch Effect" didn't just empty supermarket shelves.

In response to this growing phenomenon, and given a Mario mushroom boost thanks to the 2020 global pandemic lockdowns, across the globe, more and more stay-at-home women were gaining digital fanbases for their cleaning, cooking, DIYing, couponing and parenting. As of summer 2023, #cleantok had 83 billion views on the video app TikTok, and this is joined by the growing practice of homesteading, in which users (in the overwhelming majority, women) share snippets of their lives made simpler by living off their land, homeschooling and crafting their own home staples from bread to soap.

There's also the added layer that people can't help but consume content which makes them feel shit about themselves. I deleted the TikTok app during my second maternity leave. Whilst scrolling through reams of beautiful women in their sparkling homes, making jam in floaty Free People dresses with their Arian home-educated children, I happened to glance up at a kitchen which never stays tidy or clean for longer than 3 minutes, to see the dog licking the baby's spit up off his belly whilst my toddler ground raspberries into his hair. It is a feral scene that brings me joy and comfort, and as much as my human instinct aches to draw comparisons between my home and the homes I see on my thumb-wanders, I refuse to allow it. But it's very easy and very common for people to feel like they're not holding their lives together when they see millions of examples of those who seemingly are.

One need not venture far into the comments sections of these videos to see the projections from hurt people (hurt only by themselves in their act of internalising the content they've viewed). In a self-timed one minute of looking at 'cleantok' and homestead videos, I came across the following comments. "Step 1, be rich", "You must be so bored", and "Honestly, why bother?". If we can't safeguard ourselves from viewing the content that triggers our insecurities, should we at least learn to self-regulate after viewing something that makes us feel shitty? If creators are flocking to the internet en masse to upload content to make themselves feel

Click Me Baby One More Time…

validated and connected, but watching said content makes the viewer feel invalidated and disconnected, we find ourselves in a paradox.

One could argue that these trends offer worldwide visibility and appreciation for a woman's work in the home and that the women who create and share this content are leaders of progress and empowerment. Thanks to social media, women's work within the home is evolving. In my household, the toolbox and power saw are my pride and joy (a tradesman once admired some of my carpentry whilst commenting on my husband's "soft, desk job hands"), and I learned all of my building skills and confidence from other women on the internet.

Work Bitch

Work Bitch

"Such a girl boss!" The comments came flooding in as I announced the official launch of my marketing agency in the spring of 2020. "Boss babe" and "#ladyboss", they read one after another. I knew that people meant well; their words were charged with excitement and genuine encouragement, but they left me with mixed feelings. Five years previously, when my now husband founded his property tech startup, the messages of support didn't come with a qualifier. His hard work, tenacity and courage were applauded at face value, the term "boss" being deemed independently acceptable because he's male.

I grew up in a household of four strong women (including the cats), and our toolbox was as frequently used as our baking scales. My mother worked full-time in a highly skilled field in IT, and due to these factors, I didn't perceive any limitations based on gender. However, it was during my teen years, specifically in preparation for Year 8 careers week, that I was first introduced to workplace politics. Alongside two friends, I eagerly submitted my dream work experience application in the media field, envisioning a future as a director or producer. On receiving our placements, the response read, "Unfortunately, we have been unable to find a suitable local placement in this field, so we have enrolled you in an alternative placement which we hope you will find equally enriching". My friends (it now feels appropriate to share that they are both male) had been signed up to shadow a local software development team for their work experience week, which I was still excited about! I opened my letter to reveal my auto-enrollment in… a toddler nursery.

Click Me Baby One More Time...

Over the years, we have witnessed a shift in society's attitudes towards the career opportunities available to women. Initiatives have emerged, aiming to bridge the gender gap in fields like STEM and professional sport, and it's more common now than ever to see women in leadership positions. As with almost every social change movement, major brands have embraced the opportunity to launch campaigns with powerful women at the forefront, like Barbie's *Female Founders* dolls and Nike's *Dream Crazier* campaign. Two significant events in my annual calendar as a marketeer have always been Mother's Day and International Women's Day, where the pressure to present as a progressive and empowering brand is usually matched by the massive budgets invested to fulfil that goal. Often, the hopes for creating a positive social impact are drowned out by the calls for a solid return on investment.

While these developments in theory represent progress, they have also created a new phenomenon: the toxic 'girl boss' culture. While the term may initially seem gender-specific, its influence extends beyond the experiences of women. Hustle culture, with its emphasis on relentless work and the glorification of productivity, affects individuals of all genders. The rise of girl boss culture, focusing on female empowerment and entrepreneurial spirit, reflects a broader societal shift towards redefining success and challenging traditional gender roles. However, both phenomena are deeply intertwined with the prevailing values of our capitalist society, where work and productivity define our worth. The pressure to hustle and to constantly strive for more reinforces a work culture that prioritises achievement at the expense of personal well-being and genuine fulfilment.
-

The power suits with shoulder pads, aggressive blush and perms of the 70s and 80s professional woman gave way to a new era of businesswoman - the Girl Boss. This She-EO, Mompreneur movement suddenly set the bar very high for women. As comedian

Work Bitch

Ali Wong satirically puts it, "Feminism is the worst thing that ever happened to women. Our job used to be no job." Now, we are being asked to "Lean In" and work hard to prove ourselves more and more.

After an early career in politics, Sheryl Sandberg grew Google's ad team from four people to 4,000. In 2007, she was snapped up by Mark Zuckerberg to be the first COO of Facebook, a position she still held when I wrote this chapter in 2022. In 2013, she published Lean In, a nonfiction exploration into a lack of women in leadership positions, intending to inform and inspire. The book certainly made waves - it rode the New York Times bestseller list for over a year, and in 2018, it had sold 4.2 million copies, with around 12,000 still selling every month. It contains some excellent observations and advice, tackling imposter syndrome and sexual discrimination and suggests that gender equality in leadership has the power to benefit all members of society. She states, "Our culture needs to find a robust image of female success that is first, not male, and second, not a white woman on the phone, holding a crying baby". Right on, sister (although 'success' for me for the early years of parenthood has primarily embodied the latter). However, we can't ignore the misogynistic tones running through her work. Her advice suggests that women create barriers for themselves by conforming to gender stereotypes and typical gender roles. For example, she advises women entering salary negotiations to openly acknowledge "that women often get paid less than men" and to adopt "we" pronouns instead of "I" so as not to appear selfish and brash. I'd argue that for women to find equal opportunities for success, it's not our palatability that needs to change, but instead, the patriarchal systems and the acceptance of our individuality.

Some other common criticisms of Sandberg and her "feminist" work identify that she fails to acknowledge the barriers put in place for mothers and for ambitious women who don't start on the same level playing field as a middle-class, white, non-disabled cit-het woman. There's also the hypocrisy of a woman telling other women to "lean in" to find success but leading the operations at a multi-billion-dollar corporation with a history of misogyny (as of 2020, 63% of Facebook employees were male, and average pay and bonuses for women at Facebook UK that same year were 5.1%, and 41.8% lower than men, respectively.)

Sophia Amoruso founded the fast fashion brand Nasty Gal in 2006, aged just 22. Six years into trading, it was named one of "the fastest growing companies" by Inc. Magazine, and four years after that, Amoruso was named one of the wealthiest self-made women by Forbes. During her rise to success, she coined the term #GirlBoss (bear with me) and published a book by the same name with Penguin in 2014. She sold half a million copies and launched a series with Netflix, but despite her success, Sophia Amoruso is arguably far from a feminist icon. The advice within the book itself ranges from "be a nice person at work" to "don't have sex with everyone in the world you work in". She also fails to acknowledge that her whiteness and pretty privilege played a role in her rise to success in a way that isn't accessible to everyone - she sweet-talked her way out of prosecution when she was caught stealing items to sell on and was her own model when she first began selling clothes online, not something every aspiring entrepreneur could connect with. More problematic than her business advice, however, is her business. In 2015, a lawsuit appeared alleging Nasty Gal illegally terminated three women after becoming pregnant and one employee who was set to go on paternity leave. The company holds a rating of 2.6 / 5 on Glassdoor with only 19% approval of the CEO, and in 2016, the business filed for bankruptcy, being bought out by Boohoo Group after Amoruso stepped down as CEO.

In 2022, Love Island star and fashion brand Pretty Little Thing's Creative Director Molly-Mae Hague was crucified online for her appearance on the podcast Diary of a CEO, in which she stated we all have "the same 24 hours in a day" and "you're given one life, and it's up to you what you do with it". In 2023, after becoming a mum, Molly-Mae stepped down as Creative Director. There may be 24 hours in every day, but that time looks very different when you have dependents, no support and are functioning on low sleep.

As a generation, Millennials have witnessed seismic shifts in the economic and technological landscapes. As an eleven-year-old, I would phone my friend's landline on a Friday night to arrange a time to meet outside the Woolworths in town the following morning. There was no way of letting them know if I were running late or needed to cancel; I just had to show up. Within a year, the whole school was on social media platforms. A year after that, personal mobile phones, even for schoolchildren, had become commonplace, and by the time I left secondary school, almost every waking moment was spent either texting, chatting on MSN, or posting to Facebook. We are the generation that grew up with cassette players and came of age with iTunes (or Limewire) collections in the thousands. Who came home from school to four TV channels and came home from university to an infinite internet of content. It's no wonder we so often reach for nostalgia as a comfort, with F.R.I.E.N.D.S., Destiny's Child and Chuck Taylors reminding us of simpler times.

Unlike previous generations who could rely on a linear path of higher education leading to secure employment and long-term stability, millennials have encountered an uncertain and daunting economic reality. Our degrees, unless in specialised fields like law or medicine, no longer guarantee success. Instead, we grapple with student debt, struggle to find affordable housing, and face limited job prospects. Dubbed the 'generation rent,' we found ourselves living at home in our twenties, yearning for the financial security and stability that seemed within reach for our predecessors.

These economic circumstances have driven millennials to seek alternative avenues for income generation, giving rise to hustle culture and the gig economy. In a world where traditional job security is elusive, we are drawn to the promise of flexible work and the potential for multiple income streams. The gig economy allows us to monetise our skills and passions, providing a glimmer of hope in an increasingly challenging job market. The advent of the digital age and the rise of social media have created unprecedented opportunities for self-expression and entrepreneurship. However, this era of boundless connectivity has also fostered a hyper-competitive environment where personal success is often equated with exceptionalism and the relentless pursuit of financial gain. This shallow perspective can undermine the value of other forms of fulfilment, such as caregiving, community engagement, and, most importantly, personal well-being. The Wall Street Journal dubbed Millennials The Therapy Generation, with more folks my age seeking professional support to navigate childhood trauma, relationship crises and professional burnout than any other generation. One of the leading factors of this emotional degradation is the Millennial obsession with monetising our hobbies and special interests. The influence of gig economy platforms and online marketplaces has further fueled the drive to monetise every aspect of life, blurring the lines between personal passions and profit-driven endeavours.

As a teenager, I supplemented my weekend job income by freelancing online in basic blog design, video editing for YouTubers and copywriting through online skills marketplaces. I genuinely enjoyed most of these "gigs", except perhaps the copywriting job, which required me to write a 1,000-word article on why I prefer Halkidiki olives over any other kind (having actually never willingly eaten an olive in my life at that point). In my twenties, I sold various crafts on sites like Etsy and eBay, from custom T-shirts to macramé plant holders. During a stint of unhealthy coping mechanisms on my first maternity leave, I operated a local enterprise upcycling damaged charity shop furniture and reselling them on Facebook Marketplace for a profit.

I first met my husband when I was 19 years old. Through a university coursemate, I had learned of a local tech journalism startup hiring freelance copywriters in various niches, and, with my incessant need to increase my revenue streams, I applied. The founders were second-year students, one being the guy I'd end up marrying and the other a friend of his from his freshers year. What had begun as a late-night pipe dream between two enthusiastic and competent mates quickly grew in popularity, secured funding, formal office space and a growing team (which I'd manage to strongarm my way into despite a failed initial interview). The business concept had legs, and with my husband as a tech genius and budding entrepreneur and his charming partner who could lay on persuasion like butter on a crumpet, the pair were set to join the ranks of many university hustle success stories. That is until my husband got a call one day from a supplier notifying him of a missed payment. He checked the accounts to find them completely cleared, and his business partner was nowhere to be found.

This story isn't a unique one, as the allure of the glitz and capital -as perpetuated by social media- draws in narcissists and egomaniacs, outliers and the disenfranchised like moths to a flame, only to result in an Icarus-sequence demise. Is this incessant need to monetise and commodify a genuine desire for financial independence and self-determination, or have societal pressures and the need for validation created a culture that values *hustle* above all else? As millennials strive to escape the shackles of traditional career paths and corporate hierarchies, they find themselves caught in a new trap—a trap that often disregards the value of collective action, community engagement, and personal well-being. What are the limitations of a system that rewards financial wealth and professional accolades at the expense of holistic fulfilment? Is personal success truly achievable within a capitalist framework? And can pursuing individual empowerment inadvertently perpetuate existing power structures and societal biases?

Click Me Baby One More Time…

The rise of social media has heightened the pressures and anxieties associated with hustle culture. The curated highlight reels on platforms like Instagram and LinkedIn present a distorted reality where success is measured by likes, followers, and external validation. The constant comparison to others' perceived achievements fuels a relentless cycle of self-doubt, burnout, and the never-ending quest for more. A recruiter friend once told me that she struggles to place talented Millenials in a specific set of businesses because, and she quotes, "the brand won't look good on my LinkedIn". What does the future look like for a generation that collects sexy, trendy corporations like Pokémon gym badges and rejects roles with potentially better training opportunities, salary packages, and well-being benefits? What does it mean to find genuine fulfilment in a world obsessed with hustle and relentless pursuit?

My twenties were spent in a London full of entrepreneurship and individualism ideology. The most successful podcasts, Twitter accounts and books preached the hustle mindset, and prominent figures on social media perpetuated this as they strived to diversify their revenue streams and increase their "offline" reach. During this time, coworking spaces such as We Work were on the rise, filled to the brim with budding young wannabe Forbes 30 under 30 alums and churning out startups all vying to be the next Facebook and Uber. My first grad job was on the marketing team for a charity that was partnered with a Google venture called Google Campus, a coworking space, conference venue and all-around entrepreneur's haven tucked away in Bonny Shoreditch. I spent the majority of my time there supporting student and graduate entrepreneurs.

Sitting in a pub in many London districts such as Peckham, Hackney and Camden, you can enjoy the view of a seemingly thriving working-class micro-community. Cheap, independent "cafs" and chicken shops line the high streets, the bustling markets are full of first-generation immigrants and lifelong Londoners alike, and the young folk who pass you by are dressed in second-hand clothes, rolling their own cigarettes and carrying furniture they've recently rescued from a roadside skip. Yet despite these boroughs having a reputation for high levels of poverty and crime, Lambeth and Hackney each have the highest number of residents in London who are educated to a degree level or higher. The average income for Lambeth residents in 2021 was £44,000, 15% higher than the average national wage in the UK. Despite appearances, the majority of Peckham's residents are middle-class millennial high-earners, borrowing the aesthetic of their homes, clothes and lifestyle from those on the poverty line.

Is this borrowing of aesthetic and lifestyle choices by middle-class millennials an attempt to establish a sense of authenticity, a way to distance oneself from the perceived superficiality of mainstream consumer culture? How does this phenomenon intersect with gentrification and the displacement of long-standing communities? Does it represent a genuine appreciation for working-class culture, or does it risk perpetuating stereotypes and erasing the struggles faced by these communities?

As peoples' lives and personal brands are ever more broadcast through digital platforms, where users seek to portray themselves as unique, relatable, and connected to authentic experiences, the working-class aesthetic, with its emphasis on simplicity, thriftiness, and community, aligns with the desire for an alternative to the polished and seemingly unattainable images often promoted by mainstream influencers.

The rise of digital thrifting platforms like Vinted and Depop has disrupted the fashion space, creating new avenues for buying and selling second-hand clothing. While these platforms offer opportunities for sustainable fashion practices and unique style exploration, they have bred a large community of opportunistic resellers. These individuals often scour local markets, thrift stores, and charity shops for vintage and unique pieces that they can then resell at a significant markup online, leading to a shift in the accessibility and affordability of thrifting and pricing out those who rely on thrifting as a means of obtaining affordable clothing. As resellers curate their online shops to cater to popular demand, they inadvertently shape the market by highlighting specific styles and eroding the diversity and inclusivity that once characterised thrifting. 90s denim, sneakers and jackets used to sit untouched and cheaply priced in the back of dusty charity shops, but thanks to celebrities, fashion houses and digital influencers popularising their aesthetic, these retro pieces are now marked up to luxury prices.

Similarly, hustle culture is borrowed and glamorised by the wealthy and privileged from those who needed to hustle because they had no other choice. The glorification of relentless work and the pursuit of entrepreneurial success has become a trend embraced by those with the privilege of a safety net or access to resources that allow them to take risks and found startup after startup.

The reality is that for many, hustling is not a choice but a necessity born out of circumstances. Those who face systemic barriers, lack financial security or come from disadvantaged backgrounds often have to hustle to survive and provide for themselves and their families. However, the current portrayal of hustle culture often fails to acknowledge these underlying challenges and instead romanticises the idea of endless ambition and rapid success.

The inclusion of individuals like Kylie Jenner on the Forbes 30 Under 30 list not only challenges our definition of success but also shines a light on the influence of privilege and nepotism in the entrepreneurial world. Each year, the announcement of the list creates waves on social media, setting the zeitgeist for entrepreneurial success and accolades. Jenner's remarkable achievement of billionaire status through her social media presence and beauty empire should make us question the values and aspirations upheld by society. While her fortune is impressive, she was stripped of her title of *Youngest Self-Made Billionaire* less than a year after she was awarded it. A closer examination of Forbes' famous list highlights that Jenner isn't alone in her nepotism and privileged foundations.

A prevalent narrative paints traditional corporate jobs as inherently oppressive or soul-sucking. This perspective suggests that working for oneself is the ultimate path to freedom, personal fulfilment, and liberation from the constraints of the corporate world. On one hand, the corporate world is often criticised for its rigid hierarchies, bureaucracy, and focus on profit maximisation. Many people feel trapped within the corporate machine, where their individuality and creative expression may be stifled. On the other hand, the pursuit of entrepreneurship is associated with the promise of autonomy, self-determination, and the ability to shape one's destiny. The idea that *doing what you love means you'll never work a day in your life* is appealing and suggests that self-employment holds the key to true happiness and fulfilment.

However, working for oneself does not automatically guarantee liberation or eliminate the challenges of the labour market. Entrepreneurs and self-employed folks face their own set of pressures, including financial risks, long working hours, and the need to be really quite good at a number of business specialisms as well as whatever it is they're actually selling. The idea that you're only working for *the man* if you're employed by a corporation seems to disregard the possibility that *the man* can take many forms, such as investors, clients, customers and the tax man.

The layperson's misconceptions surrounding being "your own boss" are often shaped by the glamorisation and idealisation of entrepreneurship in online spaces. The allure of financial freedom, flexibility, and the ability to create one's own destiny can be captivating and is preyed on by the multi-level marketing (MLM) industry. MLMs or Pyramid Schemes often masquerade as legitimate business opportunities, offering individuals the promise of financial success and empowerment - the earliest popular form of these were AVON and the Tupperware parties of the 70s, but more recent examples include Scentsy and Herbalife (the latter of which made $5.2Bn in revenue in 2022). However, at their core, they are structured in a way that prioritises recruitment over the actual sale of products or services. Participants are often required to invest substantial amounts of money upfront and are encouraged to recruit others into the scheme to earn commissions.

Social media has become a powerful tool for MLMs to target and groom potential recruits. Platforms like Instagram and Facebook are teeming with posts that showcase lavish lifestyles, extravagant vacations, and testimonials of financial success, all supposedly achieved through participation in the MLM. These posts create an illusion of prosperity and entice individuals seeking a way out of financial difficulties or desiring a sense of community and support. The majority of participants end up experiencing economic loss, as the pyramid structure inherently benefits only those at the top. The emphasis on recruitment often leads to saturated markets and unsustainable business practices. Many individuals find themselves trapped in a cycle of debt and dependency, struggling to make ends meet while their superiors profit from their efforts.

For some people, successful entrepreneurship is doing what many wouldn't dare to do. It's early Autumn in 2021, and I'm sitting on a Zoom call alone, waiting for Bella to join me characteristically late to discuss a contract I'm currently working on for the business she founded. In all of our previous virtual meetings, she's been direct yet mousey, bare-faced with her hair scraped back and glasses covering half of her lovely face. Bella is younger than me, that isn't her real name -it's a stage alter ego- and she makes up to £7K a month. The screen flickers to life, and my dreary Hampshire view is instantly ridiculed by the paradise taking up her half of the screen. She comes into the frame, unrecognisable as a total glamazon - tanned, face and hair made up like she's about to walk the runway and with a *famous* air about her. She's on set in Dubai, ready to spend a day in front of the camera shooting for her next few months of work. She's not a movie star or a model; Bella is an OnlyFans creator.

Launching in 2016, the platform OnlyFans was built as a way for creators to paywall their content. By 2022, it had over 170 million users, with an average of half a million joining daily. I recently spent a year working with the leading network for OnlyFans creators, run by OnlyFans creators, which rejects the stigmas that the platform is a pornographic site. Whilst it's true that some creators on the platform produce X-rated content, in reality, the majority of content is suggestive at best. Most importantly, OnlyFans protects and empowers its predominantly female creator base. Women rule on OnlyFans. Male creators on the platform earn 60 cents for every dollar earned by women. The platform only takes 20% of the creator's revenue, and there are significant tech advantages in place, such as intellectual property protections (all content uploaded is copyrighted to the creator) and restrictions on the recording and screenshotting of content within the platform. The top 3 earners on the platform in 2021 were women, making a combined income of over $40 million per month through earnings on OnlyFans.

If you compare OnlyFans to the adult video industry, which has always notoriously been dominated by men and exploitative of women, or even traditional creator platforms like YouTube and Instagram, which make it difficult to protect IP (all Instagram users sign a waiver granting Meta a "non-exclusive, fully paid and royalty-free, transferable, sub-licensable, worldwide licence to use their content") and make a decent living (The average YouTube channel receives around $0.018 per ad view) it's difficult not to see the appeal for female creators who want autonomy and protection over their content businesses.

Click Me Baby One More Time…

One of the most successful OnlyFans models in the UK (let's call her Ellie) receives hundreds of messages per day from men offering to pay between £20 and £250 for a single private suggestive image. The frequency of these orders increases the more that she engages in flirty chat with them. Only, it isn't her doing the dirty talk. Ellie walked me through her business model, which is only scalable to meet demand thanks to the support of her brother and mum, who work full time in the DMs of her OnlyFans account, masquerading as Ellie. The same single image is often sold to many, many multiples of fans, leading to tens of thousands of pounds of potential profit from one photo.

The emergence of social media platforms challenges traditional notions of entrepreneurship and raises essential questions about the nature of work and success in our society. They provide a space for everyday people to monetise their content and gain financial independence on their terms. While these platforms offer opportunities for individuals to find autonomy and economic success outside of traditional corporate structures, creators face constant pressure to produce and maintain a steady stream of content, often creating videos and images to cater to their subscribers' and brand partners' desires and expectations.

The rise of platforms like OnlyFans raises broader questions about the commodification of intimacy, the influence of social media on our perceptions of success, and the blurred boundaries between work and personal life. The glamour and allure of the "girl boss" or "entrepreneur" lifestyle portrayed on social media can mask the challenges and sacrifices that come with running a business or being self-employed. It is crucial to critically examine the narratives and representations presented to us and question whether these ideals align with our personal values and aspirations. How do we define success, and how do we determine which aspirations are our own and which are borrowed from our time spent scrolling? What are the long-term implications of building personal brands heavily reliant on algorithms and user engagement metrics?

Pretty Woman

Pretty Woman

The everyday internet user is growing increasingly aware of their digital footprint, where every keystroke, swipe and click leaves a virtual trace on servers and the sites and apps we interact with. But what about the impact our digital acts are making on the offline world and ourselves? Human history has long valued personal appearance and identity, but the digital age has intensified this quest for validation, making self-image a key driver in the everyday decisions that we make. We each find ourselves on a global stage, where how we present ourselves and our lives can have a powerful impact on our social standing, relationship and career opportunities and our legacy. Our personal brand, be this as simple as through the holiday we brag about on Facebook to our closest friends and family, the dating profile we curate, or the public Instagram account we own to showcase our crochet vegetable enterprise, gives us control over how the world perceives us. Through our online activity, we directly or subconsciously seek recognition, connection and perhaps even a hint of immortality. We willingly -if often naively- offer up our personal data as currency to allow us access to this world, and then once inside, the way we look, the thoughts we think and the things we achieve become the points system deciding our position in society.

The 21st Century has ushered in an unprecedented era of data-driven influence, where every interaction adds to the vast reservoir of information that shapes the content we consume and create. Our desires are observed, moulded and commoditised, and amongst many things, this impacts our perception of beauty. The allure of acceptance and admiration prompts a curation of self-image, often formed by popular trends and ever-shifting beauty standards. Many find themselves caught between social pressure to be beautiful, interesting and aspirational whilst yearning for authenticity and genuine connection. Others find their true, offline selves unable to keep up with the version of themselves they present online, where their conversation responses can be considered and edited, their appearance can be filtered, and the images of their experiences and lifestyle can be curated to show only the highlights.

But as the opportunities to impress grow, so do the risks of being criticised. The more we share online and the wider audience we reach, the more we open ourselves up to the mass inquisition of the digital populous. Most of us are no stranger to scrutiny. Your mum hates your new haircut, your father-in-law has strong opinions about the way you grill sausages, and your boss warns that your timekeeping needs improvement, and you may respond to these with varying degrees of don't-give-a-single-shit to consumes-every-waking-thought. Generally, the comments that sting the most are the ones that relate to our innermost insecurities, often even more so when they come from strangers. A 2010 UK study amongst children showed that those with higher self-esteem weren't necessarily bullied less than those with low self-esteem but that the lasting effects of bullying were acute and minimal.

To a lot of people, physical appearance is a powerful tool. We've found evidence of body customisation in ancient cultures worldwide, and today, piercings, tattoos, fashion and makeup are still significant cultural markers, expressions of identity, and, in some cases, armour for how we choose to present ourselves in society. A beard, acrylic nails, or a particular jacket might serve as insulation for when you feel underconfident. I have what loved ones affectionately (I think) refer to as my "drag persona", the version of me who wears false lashes, heavy face contour, big hair and sparkly heels, reserved for moments in my career where I'm required to speak on stage or screen, and when I'm usually feeling my most vulnerable and anxious.

Pretty Woman

Our bodies and physical identities are deeply personal, and the advent of social media has meant that strangers can hide behind their screens while passing public judgment on others' appearances. But the critique doesn't exclusively come from internet users; it filters down from above - the algorithms and the tech giants who build them.

In the USA, the *land of the free,* some states such as Indiana and Kentucky have specific laws ruling against the public exposure of *female* nipples specifically. In Europe, in the eyes of the law, women have equal rights to men when it comes to public nudity and indecency offences. However, most European nudity laws stipulate that a woman's breasts are only considered legally "decent" if their exposure does not cause public outrage or arousal. I don't know about you, but in my experience growing up a woman in Britain, I've been led to believe that any exposure of a woman's breasts is considered outrageous and/or arousing. Our newspapers and magazines are riddled with female body sexualisation, critique and comparison. On our beaches, in our sports stadiums, and on our screens, there are male nipples aplenty and rarely a female nipple in sight.

The irony that I'm writing this chapter while sheepishly breastfeeding my newborn son in a cafe is not lost on me. 23% of Americans indicate they would be "somewhat or very uncomfortable" with a woman breastfeeding near them. In a recent maternal survey in Scotland, more than a quarter of mums admitted to being made to feel uncomfortable for attempting to feed their children in public. In 2017, children's publisher Usborne was forced to apologise for a passage in one of their educational books that read that breasts exist to make girls look "grown-up and attractive". Yikes. It's no wonder we women feel uncomfortable exposing our torsos as freely as men do when these perpetuated stigmas surround us.

Click Me Baby One More Time…

And it's not just a UK issue; Meta (reaching 3.45 billion people monthly across their products in 2021) has faced endless scrutiny for censoring female nipples across their platforms and leaving male nipples to live as they please online.

This algorithmic bias -systematic and repeatable errors that create unfair outcomes, such as privileging one arbitrary group of users over others- affects plus-sized black women more than any other group. In 2020, model Nyome Nicholas-Williams was threatened with a ban from Instagram when she uploaded a portrait (shot by Alexandra Cameron) in which she has her arms wrapped around her naked chest. "Millions of pictures of very naked, skinny white women can be found on Instagram every day," said Nicholas-Williams. "But a fat black woman celebrating her body is banned? I feel like I'm being silenced." Another plus-sized black creator, Stephanie Yeboah, lobbied Meta directly regarding this issue, and this, combined with a petition garnering 23,000 signatures to "stop Instagram from censoring fat Black women," forced the platform to change its policy on semi-nudity and retrain the staff responsible for the algorithm and the platform's review process.

The historical public perception of female bodies is an unlucky dip, and each cultural shift brings new societal rules on what is deemed acceptable. Between the 15th and 18th centuries, European royals were often painted with their breasts exposed. Just imagine the scandal if Kate and Meghan solicited topless photoshoots. It's often said that in Victorian England, ankles were considered too sexy to show. Yet, only a few generations later, men of today seem to control themselves just fine around women with their ankles exposed.

Of 191 different cultures globally, breasts are considered sexually significant to men in only 13. In fact, in many cultures, the idea that a woman's breasts would be held as an object of sexual pleasure is considered perverted and unnatural. So why is it that in the 21st-century Western world, my husband and sons can enjoy the public pool sans top, and I cannot? The answer lies in systems of control.

-

The disparaging public reception of OnlyFans combines the need to police women's bodily autonomy with a historical disdain for financially independent women. We talked earlier about the sex workers of the 19th Century, who were unjustly blamed for the spread of Victorian venereal diseases while their male customers were overlooked. Today's creators face similar scapegoating, being hailed as the root of societal issues such as the self-image crisis and the upholding of dated, seedy male entertainment industries, while the other half of the equation—the willing and engaging customers—escape scrutiny. These creators are merely supplying a service driven by demand, and the customer is always right, right?

In a commodity economy, who truly drives the demand? Is it the customer, or is it the supplier? I have spent the last decade sitting within the marketing teams at some of the biggest consumer brands in the world. I have pored over the cycle, where consumer insights inform the products a brand produces while simultaneously investing unthinkable sums of money to stimulate and manipulate demand for those products. It is a game of influence, where desires are both observed and shaped and where market trends are analysed and exploited.

As technologies have advanced, so too has the depth of available data on consumers. If you've ever felt like the ads you see when you scroll result from your phone listening to you, that's because it is. But not through the microphone, earwigging on your conversations; no, your phone is listening to your behaviour. Your maps app knows where you're travelling from and to, your browser knows which websites are your favourites and which questions you need answers to, and your social media app knows who you spend time with and who inspires you. Every time you access your device, you feed it more and more information about what makes you tick and what makes you click. A director at Google once told me that

Click Me Baby One More Time...

Google knows your partner is going to propose to you before he does.

Corporations, when armed with this information, endeavour to tap into these depths, leveraging emotional triggers, social aspirations, and even insecurities to create a demand that might not have existed before. Through meticulously crafted advertising campaigns, celebrity endorsements, and strategic brand positioning, the supplier moulds the desires and aspirations of the customer, framing their products as the answer to unmet needs and the gateway to a better life.

The more predictable you become, the easier you are to sell to. Digital creators wield a similar power on a much smaller scale. The "back end" of a creator's social media page provides them with a wealth of information about who is consuming their content - the demographics such as gender and age, usage such as at what times of day their audience is most likely to be scrolling online, and engagement metrics such as which types of content get the most likes, shares and convert the most sales. Some external tools even offer deeper and arguably less ethical insights into customers, such as their predicted salary band and ethnicity based on the accounts they follow and the products they buy. A savvy creator will use this information to direct the content they produce, controlling the likelihood of sustained positive engagement and increasing their earning power.

With this plethora of data and the layers of control over what is and isn't being delivered to our screens, who holds the reins of influence over our self-image and desires? Is it the algorithms that meticulously curate our content feeds, the corporations that leverage our data to shape our aspirations or the creators who mould their offerings based on our every click?

I was born in 1993, so my early adolescence was dominated by Myspace, Bebo and MSN Messenger. Whilst these brought their own political landscape to navigate, self-expression and image curation were largely related to one's personal brand - the music you listened to, the celebs you fancied and the pop culture niches you subscribed to. Social media was like looking at the early 2000s high school teen movie cafeteria trope and then deciding which table you would sit at; the jocks, the goths or the band geeks. These platforms and other web-based spaces like Tumblr and Geocities allowed users to customise every element of their personal pages, from background colours to fonts to the music played when someone viewed their profile. The goal wasn't to appear perfect; it was to demonstrate your personality as it related to cultural signifiers.

By the time I graduated from university, Facebook and Instagram had culturally buried their predecessors, and, as they didn't offer the functionality for users to brand their corner of the platform, the onus was all on the content that users were posting to demonstrate who they were and what they stood for. In my early twenties, working in the beauty industry and therefore surrounded by beautiful and interesting people, I quickly felt the pressure to curate my personal brand through my social media pages. The vanity born in historical society but amplified by 21st-century social platforms has forced a culture of comparison and self-critique like never before. Those who post on social media seek constant validation, usually validation for versions of themselves that don't actually exist. As somebody who not only grew up alongside an emerging internet world but has actively contributed to that world almost every day for the past 18 years, I've experienced firsthand the highs and lows of the digital ego.

-

At 22, I had just landed a dream job at a boutique content marketing agency, specialising in *influencer* campaigns and events. My role was to take on contracts from big brands like Selfridges, GHD and Penguin Random House, and find content creators who could promote new products on their social media channels for a fee, then manage the relationship with those creators to ensure that the content was landing all of the right messages and achieving the KPIs set by the brand.

One Spring day, whilst on a campaign shoot in Paris, I started to upload a selfie I had taken with some of the models on set. Instagram was still relatively novel to me, but my boss had assured me that I needed to be active on the platform to represent the agency well. A Belgian model with eerily poreless skin leaned over my shoulder and, scrunching up her nose, said, "Please whiten my teeth before you post that". *Whiten her teeth??* I thought. I instinctively looked at the real-life mouth before me and saw nothing but dead, straight, bone-china-white teeth. I looked back at the picture on my phone screen and saw the same beautiful set smiling back at me. My second thought was that if she wanted them any whiter, it was too late now as the image had already been taken and was sitting in my hand with nary a dentist about. My thoughts were interrupted when another of the girls appeared behind me (towering over me like a floating gazelle). She jabbed at my iPhone, "Can you blur my arm too, please? That shadow makes it look weird". I couldn't see anything wrong with either of her arms or any part of her, to be honest. All of the girls in the photo looked amazing. Getting impatient with the stupid expression on my face, the first girl took my phone from my hand and started scrolling through my apps. "Where do you keep FaceTune?" She asked simply. When I didn't respond, she explained to me, "FaceTune? It's an editing app." She downloaded it for free on my phone, and within 60 seconds, she handed it back to me, telling me to "post that one" before turning back to the girl who was styling her weave.

I stared at the photo in my hand. It didn't look any different to me, but I followed the model's lead (she was objectively more remarkable than I'd ever be) and uploaded it with some witty caption along the lines of "bitches in Paris *peace hand sign emoji*". Throughout the evening, I experienced the still new but increasingly exciting warm flutter each time a notification popped up to tell me that someone had "liked" or "commented" on my photo. About a dozen comments in total from acquaintances and strangers fawning over my *dream job* and swanky new lifestyle, my life seemingly unrecognisable from my very humble and decidedly less glamorous previous 21 years on earth. One comment stood out to me. "You look incredible *heart eyes*" from a girl who had been in my year at school. In fact, she'd been one of the hot girls who didn't ever speak to me at school. I scrolled back up to look at the photo - I *did* look quite good; she was right. I'd always been self-conscious about my teeth, but here they looked passable, my skin was smooth, and my eyes sparkled. This *rubbing shoulders with models* business was clearly leaving its mark!

I exited Instagram and opened my photos app to look at the other images from the shoot, and my heart dipped a little as I flicked through, unable to find one I was as confident with as that selfie with all the girls. I landed on the original photo, and my thumb paused. At first glance, it was the same as the uploaded picture, but I could tell that it wasn't. I swiped across, and the image saved from FaceTune by the model appeared. I flicked between the two, searching for the dissimilarities like a primary school *spot the difference* worksheet. I couldn't believe what I was seeing - almost every single one of our features had been altered in some way. Our eyes and smiles had been given more detail and brightened and whitened. The skin on our faces and arms had been smoothed. As I looked closer, I noticed that a barely visible makeup-covered spot had disappeared from one of the girls' chins, as had a stray hair from another's forehead. And did we look slightly taller, too? How had she made so many edits in such a short amount of time?

Over the weeks and months, I found myself becoming more and more critical of every image I saw of myself. Spotting imperfections I had never noticed before, the zoom function on my phone screen made it possible to first identify and then erase even the finest of fine lines and pores on my very young skin. The owner of the agency (and my boss) was an incredibly successful and industry-trailblazing influencer herself, and she held informal workshops for the team, showing us the tips and tricks of easy image editing. At the same time, thanks to the work events I was attending and the product samples I was fortunate enough to be gifted, I became increasingly interested in makeup. I'd pore over fashion magazines and replay "Werk Room" scenes in Ru Paul's Drag Race (where the queens would do their makeup and bitch to each other). I'd sometimes spend hours applying product after product to my face, perfecting my application techniques and then snap a selfie to share on my Instagram page. Each time, I'd find myself disappointed in my phone's mere 8-megapixel inability to truly capture how the makeup looked. I'd use apps to correct each selfie, adjusting the colours and the shapes of the makeup on my face until they reflected what I saw in the mirror. I also started to make other adjustments too. I'd learned how to visually straighten my teeth by painting over the shadows cast by the uneven spacing. To enlarge my eyes to appear more doe-like. To swell my top lip to better match my bottom in a way I could not achieve with makeup. Before I knew it, every image I uploaded to social media had to undergo half an hour of rigorous editing before the girl in the photo looked like the girl I wanted to present to the world.

I look back at those photos now, and they make me sad. I don't recognise that girl at all, and besides, they are very clearly edited, so it's likely I wasn't fooling anyone except myself. I didn't consciously stop, either; I just slowly, over time, became more confident in my skin and less upset by the raw person I saw on my phone screen. I also paid thousands of pounds to straighten my teeth, an act I don't regret one bit but one which I can't be sure I did for any reason other than vanity. I'm a woman who came of age in a world where image is not only currency, as it has been for generations, but where it has never been easier to scrutinise and be scrutinised. It's why we have a fast fashion epidemic, cosmetic surgery is a rising trend, and eating disorders among children are at an all-time high.

Pretty Woman

-

Our society's relentless fixation on appearance takes a heavy toll on our mental well-being and distorts our sense of reality. The constant exposure to carefully crafted images of seemingly perfect bodies, coupled with the pressure to attain a specific and ever-changing aesthetic, can lead to body dissatisfaction and the development of disordered eating patterns. Countless young girls, influenced by the images they see online, find themselves trapped in a dangerous cycle of self-hate and extreme dieting or excessive exercise. Whilst body shaming has become a cultural norm, social media has provided a platform for public scrutiny and judgement, where individuals' appearances are relentlessly picked apart and criticised. This toxic culture not only perpetuates harmful stereotypes but also fuels the destructive mindset that equates worth with appearance. A survey conducted by stem4 in 2022 revealed that an upsetting three out of four children as young as 12 express dissatisfaction with their bodies and feel embarrassed about their looks.

The algorithms employed by these platforms play a significant role in shaping our online experiences. Through machine learning, these algorithms analyse user engagement and preferences to understand their interests and align them with content that generates the most interaction. The ultimate goal of these apps is to keep users glued to their phones, scrolling and consuming for as long as possible. However, this approach reinforces existing biases and perpetuates harmful content that negatively impacts body image and mental health. Insecurities are fed as we continue to post and scroll to find the next compliment or source of validation, in turn feeding our insecurities back into this perpetual machine. Platform giants like Bytedance (TikTok) and Meta (Instagram), as major players in the social media landscape, bear a responsibility to address the consequences of their algorithmic systems.

And it's not just kids who are impacted by this. The digital revolution has transformed the beauty industry and how we, as adults, perceive ourselves and others. Social media serves as a potent tool for the beauty marketing industry to uphold and perpetuate patriarchal beauty standards. On platforms like Instagram, the flawless, filtered images promoted by influencers and beauty brands create an unattainable ideal for beauty, fueling feelings of inadequacy and promoting a narrow definition of attractiveness.

Many people are familiar with the Coco Chanel story and how, in the 1920s, she sported a tan (which was usually associated with the rural working classes as a symptom of their manual labour), which revolutionised what was considered *beautiful* among the middle and upper classes and generated an entire category of cosmetics products promising to provide that sun-kissed glow. Hollywood starlets of the 1940s and 50s did the same for lipstick sales, Twiggy in the 60s for mascara, and the supermodels of the 80s and 90s spiked popularity in complexion products, clear mascaras and lipglosses due to the models' "flawless", god-like aesthetic. Many beauty trends from the past decade have been born in the Korean beauty industry, such as multi-step skincare routines and simple, glowy makeup.

Brands inherently follow market trends to remain relevant in an ever-evolving, competitive market. Ten years ago, every cosmetics ad and beauty guru was preaching gospel about the latest matte effect liquid lipstick and anti-shine powder. Partway through my makeup brand tenure, matte was *out,* and every new product launch promised to be the glowiest and dewiest available. Early in my career, sustainable and cruelty-free brands were reserved for vegan shoppers, presumably filling their jute shopping baskets with low-performance but high-ethic products. Inclusivity did not exist, as the market was heavily segmented into mass brands (designed, operated, marketed, sold and bought by Eurocentric people) and niche brands (specialist products created, stocked and bought by BIPOC folk). Body-positive campaigns were rare and, therefore, noteworthy, such as Unilever's 2004 *Real Beauty* campaign for Dove.

There were times in the boardrooms I sat in when potential ambassadors and models were suggested and shot down on the basis that they weren't "aspirational" enough. The belief was that if they weren't the Global North's contemporary epitome of beauty, people wouldn't be inspired to buy the products they were promoting.

Yet, in recent years, we have seen a shift. Current market data shows consumers are becoming far more conscious about the brands they support with their spending choices. Suddenly, it's very uncool to buy products from unethical and unsustainable brands, and marketing teams are tripping over themselves to promote how inclusive, moral and eco-friendly they are in order to maintain and expand their slice of the profit pie (Dove saw an increase of 700% in sales following the Real Beauty ads). Of course, there genuinely are people working at these corporations who care about these values, but a few voices in a planning meeting sadly often don't mean much if the stakeholders don't agree with the initiatives.

In fact, the first time that we saw mass brands investing in and promoting products more typically favoured by black consumers was when "blackfishing" gained momentum in the 2010s. Stars such as the Kardashians and Ariana Grande, and then trickling down to beauty influencers, popularised the controversial trend, wherein they'd adopt Black aesthetic (darkening their skin, favouring Afrocentric hairstyles, buying or synthesising fuller lips and hips), creating racial ambiguity and igniting cries of appropriation. The commodification of the "ghetto" aesthetic led to increased sales of weaves, acrylic nails, and dark lip liners but not a proportionate increase in positive Black media representation or closing of the racial pay gap in modelling and influencer marketing.

Click Me Baby One More Time…

As journalist Wanna Thompson put it, "Black is cool, unless you're actually Black."

However, with recent consumer interest in positive brand values, investors and stakeholders do currently care about promoting social progress and are willing to part with the budget to do this. In a lot of cases, this is purely virtue signalling, but is this a net good for humanity if more brands invest in ethical practices, lower their carbon footprint and continue to include all races, marginalised groups and all shapes and sizes of people in their product offering and marketing, regardless of the incentive behind this? Is the risk of all of this progress falling apart once being progressive falls out of vogue again?

The beauty industry has long thrived on exploiting insecurities, capitalising on the idea of "fixing" a never-ending list of aesthetic issues with specific products. While it is encouraging to witness some strides towards ethical practices, I find myself asking: Can an industry built on profiting from insecurities ever be truly ethical?

To fully understand how we've ended up here, we need to jump back a few decades. On paper, it might be easy to assume that the 90s and 00s were all about Girl Power. We had The Spice Girls, Angela Merkel and Hermione Granger. Yet despite pop culture bursting at the seams with female representation, these decades were largely the birth of a very toxic environment that we still suffer the effects of today.

I was born in the early '90s, and like most Western millennials, I'm only starting to truly reflect on the impact '90s and early 2000s female objectification had on my self-image and the image of other women. Yes, our charts were dominated by female representation, but it was impossible for a woman to be successful in the music industry without a heavily curated image, either squeezing them into the innocent girl next door bracket (Britney) or the raunchy

Pretty Woman

"bad girl" box (when Christina struggled to compete with the former, she was rebranded to the latter).

There was exploitation galore, financial and sexual. In 1995, TLC filed for bankruptcy at the height of their fame when it was revealed that their label left them with just $0.18 each per album sale, yet backcharging them on their promotional expenses, leaving them $3.5M in debt. Ronan Farrow's investigation uncovered over a decade of sexual abuse in Hollywood at the hands of industry powers like Harvey Weinstein, which "everybody knew about" [Catch and Kill], but leaders in journalism, media and politics were covering up for their benefit.

Women were perpetually pitted against each other. Tabloids, magazines and early e-zines launched a still-epidemic campaign against the female body. In 1999, British television host Chris Evans famously interviewed Victoria Beckham, asking her, "Is your weight back to normal?" (two months after giving birth to their eldest, Brooklyn) and then WEIGHING her on TV to check, showing the result live. We were constantly bombarded with headlines letting us know how much our favourite female celebrities had let themselves go, piled on the pounds, or, heaven forbid, showed even a hint of ageing. The aforementioned Britney and Christina were not allowed to coexist without headlines such as "Now it's war" [heat Jan 2000] and J14's Apr 2000 classic "Who would win in a fight?".

In the 50 highest-grossing movies of the 90s worldwide, just 21% of top billing was of female actors (on their official release posters), with less than 3% of them featuring the woman in first position. Julia Roberts received second billing to co-star Richard Gere in Pretty Woman despite playing the main character, and Carrie-Ann Moss's name was relegated to the small print of The Matrix posters despite having just two minutes of screen time less than Lawrence Fishburn, who received top billing with Keanu

Click Me Baby One More Time…

Reeves. It's also important to note that only two women of colour -Whitney Houston and Irene Bedard- are featured on this list.

It was around this time that cartoonist Irene Bechdel created the Bechdel test. The test, in its simplest form, is a movie or TV show which:

has at least two women in it,
who talk to each other,
about something other than a man

The requirement that the two women must be named is sometimes added.

Almost every single Bond film fails this test, as does the Lord of the Rings trilogy. Some perhaps more surprising (read: less obviously macho) blockbuster films that fail to show two women having a normal conversation with each other are Ratatouille, Avatar, A Star is Born, My Best Friend's Wedding, Harry Potter and the Goblet of Fire and La La Land, to name just a few.

Some critics call the Bechdel test "dogmatic," but to me, it feels like a basic representation requirement that men needn't worry about for themselves. Women deserve to see themselves in roles where being sexy and obsessed with the leading man isn't their only character trait. When we ask the media industry to show us a "strong female character," we don't mean "give her some emotional armour and a martial arts skill"; we mean to show us a woman with as much interest and breadth to her story and character as you would a male lead.

A great example of female representation done 'right' is Kate Winslet's eponymous Mare of Easttown (2021). Mare is a female lead with a complex backstory and narrative. She is not traditionally feminine but not caricaturesquely butch, either. She has a body representative of the average middle-aged woman. When the director wanted to retouch her naked body during a sex scene and her face in promotional material, Winslet refused to allow it, saying,

Pretty Woman

"We've stopped learning how to love [our] faces because we keep covering them up with filters."

Mare is an excellent segue into how ageism only affects women and people who aren't cis+het+white in Hollywood, too. A 2016 Humana report examined the representation of characters over 60 years old in the top 100 grossing films of the same year. Just 2.7% of those were women with speaking roles! Of all characters aged 60+, just 22.9% were non-white. Lesbian and female bisexual characters did not feature at all.

More than a third of the movies did not portray a single female-speaking character over 60. Throughout the blockbuster list, a substantial majority of the male characters held senior positions in industries such as STEM, politics, law and academia. In the same data set, not a single female character was employed in STEM or any senior healthcare position, and only a tiny handful held any positions of clout in other industries. Whilst this is vastly under-representative of the realities of the world, it's likely a leading factor in why these industries are so heavily male-dominated.

The ageism in our pop culture is also apparent in the age gaps we see on screen. In her mid-twenties, Emma Stone was cast as the love interest of both Colin Firth, 53 (Magic in the Moonlight) and Sean Penn, 56 (Gangster Squad). In her early twenties, Jennifer Lawrence was also paired up with Bradley Cooper, 42 (Silver Linings Playbook) and Christian Bale, 40 (American Hustle). Bringing it back to Bond, 18 of the 25 James Bond appearances are played by an actor who is over 40, and in A View To A Kill, Roger Moore was 53 when his love interest, Bond Girl Melina Havelock (Carole Bouquet), was just 23. How likely are we to regularly see mature female protagonists top the box office?

But let's explore the age gap in reverse - Darlene Snell is a 68-year-old matriarch in the award-winning Netflix series Ozark. Her character is nuanced and elaborate, and she is in a romantic relationship with Wyatt, 18. However, in this relationship, the age difference between the characters is a regular point of conversation, as are ageist comments towards and about Darlene.

'80s and '90s kids will remember Stiffler's Mom and Stacey's Mom being core to the teen fantasy narrative. Kim Cattrall found her fame as sex-mad Samantha Jones in Sex and the City, with some of her partners being 20 years her junior. Stella Payne (Angela Bassett) "gets her groove back" by hooking up with a guy in his 20s, and who could forget the original cougar, Mrs Robinson (Anne Bancroft, The Graduate), who plays a married woman in her late 40s seducing 21-year-old Benjamin (Dustin Hoffman).

Considering these are some of the only examples of (relatively) "older" women exploring their sexuality in pop culture, it's not lost on me that the age of these women, especially in relation to their sexual exploits, is so core to their plotlines. Male actors have no trouble being cast in leading roles over the age of 40, and their love interest must be young for their sex to be palatable, yet the age gap isn't of importance to the plot. Laura Mulvey coined the phrase "the male gaze" in the 70s when she explored that patriarchal ideology dominates social and power structures in cinema and creates the gender inequality we see throughout pop culture. The majority of mainstream television and film is crafted by men. Amongst all nominations in the 2021 Academy Awards, 71% of adapted screenplays and 60% of original screenplays were written by men. 80% of editors and 100% of cinematographers were men. Men who are writing, capturing and cultivating the image of the women in the most popular and critically acclaimed films on our screens.

So, with the majority of female characters being produced by men, it's no wonder that our heroines are often scantily clad, the female love interests are vapid, young and skinny, and any auxiliary female characters exist exclusively for objectification and sexualisation with little to no power over the plot. Put simply, the male gaze shows us women in media through the eyes of heterosexual men. A favourite rainy Sunday afternoon activity of mine is reading through the Tweets of women describing themselves as a male author would (a thread started by Whitney Reynolds in 2018), full of results with hilariously horrifying accuracy.

"As she moved her strong cocoa body gleamed as if calling to the country of Africa. Her chocolate waist moved like an alluring siren calling me to crash on the rocks of her brown buttocks." @Kelechnekoff

"She was forty but could have passed for a year younger with soft lipstick and some gentle mascara. Her dress clung to the curves of her bosom, which was cupped by her bra that was under it, but over the breasts that were naked inside her clothes. She had a personality and eyes.". @JaneCaseyAuthor.

"As round as she was loud, she immediately filled the room. My first thought was that I didn't want to fuck her. My second thought was even more disturbing; she didn't seem to care. She contemplated the roundness of her own boobs and contributed something to the meeting. I missed it." @ashleyn1cole

How about some examples actually written by famous male authors:

"A mistake was made somehow in manufacturing, putting those big, womanly breasts on what would of otherwise [sic] been a perfect work, and you can see how bitter she is about it" - One Flew Over the Cuckoo's Nest, Ken Kesey.

"By the end of July, she was running six and sometimes seven miles a day, her boobs no more than nubs, her butt mostly nonexistent." - Just After Sunset, Stephen King.

"Her small breasts moved freely beneath a painted Dothraki vest", a description of Daenerys and her sentient breasts by George RR

Click Me Baby One More Time…

Martin as if the Mother of Dragons had intelligent tits which roamed about wherever they fancied.

I recently read the crime bestseller I Am Pilgrim written by Terry Hayes, in which the protagonist is the Best Ever Secret Agent Of All Time and every woman he encounters just so happens to be sexually attractive. Most women in male-written fiction seem to have "almond eyes" and "a heaving bosom". I'm not entirely sure my bosom has ever heaved, but if it has, it's certainly not the most remarkable thing about me.

In 1995, Bratta L. Ettinger published the Matrixial Gaze, upon which the foundations of the concept of the Female Gaze were formed. Where the male gaze objectifies and overly sexualises female characters, the female gaze empathises with complex female characters, giving agency and purpose to women in media beyond the "shapeliness" of their tits and ass. We can look at modern TV shows such as The Handmaid's Tale, Maid and Fleabag as examples of mainstream female characters written by women whose perspectives and experiences transcend male objectivity. These examples are significant because they heavily explore themes of sexual relationships, but not through a patriarchal lens. However, much work still needs to be done, as most emerging female characters lack intersectionality. Some of the most streamed female-led shows of the past couple of years (Bridgerton, You, Stranger Things, The Handmaid's Tale, Maid) failed to representatively explore the experiences of women of colour, queer women, disabled women and older women.

So we can see through film, TV series and books how their writers and directors hold vast amounts of power over how people see each other and how we view ourselves. Still, we often disregard how much this power is matched by the tech bosses and software developers who control our small screens and the brands and creators who produce the content on them.

Pretty Woman

The digital media machine cycles through creating and capitalising on vulnerabilities, then virtue signalling to commodify the antidote to our insecurities. Much like if a dentist were investing in the advertising of chocolate. And we each play a role in this, with every eyeball and engagement we feed the machine. Algorithms ensure that we exist in digital echo chambers, with content tailored not for our benefit but to retain our interest, benefitting the platforms and their financial partners. This system reinforces existing bias and validates our most dominant emotions.

This level of control over how we think and feel means that our interactions with digital platforms are becoming core to who we are as individuals. Our career -a source of identity and status for many and a vital source of income for most- is often intrinsically tied to our LinkedIn profiles. And we all know someone who is growing a family with a person they first met on a dating app. Is there a future where these integral elements of our lives exist offline as they did for the centuries before this one, or will technology continue to dominate every aspect of what makes us who we are and the course of our lives?

With our self-image and sense of self-worth increasingly invaded by forces beyond our control, how do we retain authenticity? And with filters and false self-representation continuing to evolve and infiltrate every corner of culture and society, will it even matter?

Click Me Baby One More Time…

Mean Girls

Mean Girls

The power of technology and digital platforms has facilitated global connections like never before, bridging gaps across continents and oceans, cultures and classes. It has provided a platform to amplify marginalised voices and drive social change. Through our digital personas, we can forge meaningful connections, share our stories, and find like-minded communities that provide a sense of belonging.

As I write this chapter, the world is watching what was one of the dominant digital forces of the past decade, Twitter, fall further out of favour with the general public (a decrease of at least 5% of its user base in 2023, whilst Meta's user base has *grown* by the same amount in the same period). The transitory nature of technology means that these platforms will naturally come and go, and with them, the communities and identities users have cultivated within their virtual walls. With all of the benefits of building relationships and selfhood online, the slow death of Twitter (and Bebo, MySpace, Vine, etc.) highlights the fragility of our digital identities and the need for diversifying our sources of connection and self-worth.

At first glance, you could be forgiven for thinking that the internet is a resource for exchanging ideas. Some refer to our current society as The Information Age, and Silicon Valley bosses will have you believe that the data they collect from you and the platforms they are growing using that data are designed to be hubs of connectivity. In reality, these days, the internet is a marketplace for identities.

Click Me Baby One More Time…

As we explored earlier, our personal brands online have become integral parts of who we are offline, and one of the driving forces behind this is the innate human need to belong. From ancient civilisations to modern societies, the desire to form connections and be part of a community has shaped what it means to be human. In tribal societies, individuals sought belongingness within their clans or tribes, where shared values, rituals, and language fostered a strong sense of unity and identity. The ancient Greeks were proud of their city-states, such as Athens or Sparta, each with its unique culture and customs, while mediaeval guilds provided a sense of belonging and protection for craftsmen and artisans. In the context of religion, since the beginning of time, people have found belongingness in their faith communities.

One way in which people strive to cultivate and present their identities is through their values and opinions. Online, these opinions are no longer confined to physical interactions, where they are often softened or even not voiced at all for fear of creating awkwardness or ruffling feathers. Using screens and the vast expanse of cyberspace as a shield for the potential fallout of baring one's true feelings, internet users are free to share any and every opinion they hold.

The more we share, the more our identities feel actualised, and the more we engage with and are validated by similar mindsets, the more connected we feel. But is how connected we feel a good indicator of how connected we actually are? Does the illusion of connection genuinely satisfy our innate human needs, or does it act as a veneer, lulling us into a false sense of belongingness whilst our innermost loneliness continues to grow?

The concept of "teenagers" as a distinct and recognisable social group is a relatively modern phenomenon that emerged in the 20th century. Before the mid-century, societies typically categorised individuals as either children or adults without a clear transitional phase.

As urban centres grew and industrialisation took hold, there was a shift in the economic landscape. The expansion of shops, bars, high streets and malls meant that young adults now had places to be employed and to spend their leisure time. With disposable income and a distinct youth culture emerging, a new social category (or, as marketeers would call it, "demographic") was born - teenagers.

This newfound freedom and access to consumer goods created a distinct identity for this age group, characterised by rebellion, exploration, and a unique set of interests and aspirations. The advent of popular culture, mass media, and the entertainment industry further cemented the idea of teenagers as a demographic with its own tastes and trends and a whole new subculture for brands and studios to market to.

In Maslow's hierarchy of needs, he suggests that once our very basic survival needs are met -food, water, shelter- the next most crucial human requirement is love and belonging - a sense of connection. His theorem argues that without these things, we can't elevate into confidence, self-esteem or self-actualisation. In other words, if we don't feel like we fit in socially, we can never truly understand or love who we are or reach our potential on planet Earth. Without connections, we can never truly be happy.

During adolescence, the prefrontal cortex, which manages planning, decision-making, personality expression, and social behaviour, undergoes dramatic changes. This process includes "synaptic pruning," causing a decline in grey matter, and "myelination" enhancing neural pathways. In simple terms, teenage brains discard less-used pathways while reinforcing practical ones for adulthood. This reorganisation drives swift shifts in social views and behaviours. As the prefrontal cortex matures, teens develop abstract thinking and external self-awareness, seeing themselves as others might. Myelination fosters empathy and self-control but can also heighten social self-consciousness.

The result of these changes is often referred to on TikTok as "main character syndrome", the concept of obsessively viewing yourself as if others are observing you. As If you are *the* main character. This self-consciousness and primitive desperation to be accepted makes teenagers the perfect subject for brands to reach. Companies cultivate trends and fandoms and package these up as commodities with multimillion-dollar campaigns behind them to market them to those who feel they need them most. It's often said that money can't buy happiness, but money can buy tickets to see your favourite band, a t-shirt displaying a famous film quote and the fastest-selling makeup palette of the year, giving students cultural markers that they belong. Money can buy you a sense of belonging, and belongingness equals happiness, right?

-

A handful of studio executives in the middle of the 20th Century saw potential in commodifying celebrity culture, and this, timed with the globalisation of media and an increase in popular movie and music, led to the infancy of the 2.6 TRILLION dollar industry we all know today as "show business". Icons like Marilyn Monroe and The Beatles became the epicentres of massive cultural phenomena, captivating the hearts and minds of adoring fans.

Norma Jean Baker, with the help of execs at 20th Century Fox, created the brand of Marilyn - she bleached and styled her hair and dialled up her sex appeal, and her image captured the imagination of an entire generation. Her films and public persona epitomised the aspirations and desires of young people during the postwar era. As Hollywood's most celebrated sex symbol, she embodied a new kind of stardom that extended beyond the silver screen and penetrated the collective consciousness of her fans. Teenagers and young adults idolised her glamorous lifestyle and aspired to emulate her sense of charm, allure and power.

Similarly, the Beatles, with their catchy popularisation of underground Black music and endearing, British, exportable personalities, ignited the worldwide craze known as "Beatlemania." The Beatles' rise to fame in the 1960s coincided with the height of teenage culture and the explosion of globalised, youth-oriented consumer markets. Older generations at the time hated everything they stood for - their music and distinct style resonated deeply with the sentiments of young people, and their massive fanbase became the prototype for modern fandoms.

The impact of both Monroe and The Beatles extended far beyond the confines of entertainment. They became symbols of a new era of rebellion, liberation, and self-expression, embraced by a generation seeking to break free from traditional norms and find solace in like-minded groups.

This was the first notable showcase of celebrity culture's power in shaping teenagers' identities and aspirations. The intense adoration and emotional investment in these cultural icons highlighted the desire for belonging and connection among young people, giving rise to a sense of community and shared experiences within these fandoms, much like the Directioners of the 2010s and the Swifties of the 2020s.

The most notable difference between Paul McCartney's fans and Taylor Swift's fans is their perceived level of connection to their idols. Whilst we can draw parallels between fans' intense emotional attachment and identification with both musicians, in the 60s' this presented as the archival videos we see of screaming, crying, and fainting young women pressed against concert barriers. Some bolder fans would crowd outside hotel rooms and stage doors, hoping for, at worst, a glimpse of and, at best, some level of physical encounter with the stars.

Click Me Baby One More Time…

In the digital era, as technology evolves and continues to shape our cultural landscape, we are exposed more than ever to the daily goings on in celebrity lives. Online tabloids and unofficial fan accounts on social media pump out images and videos of stolen private moments, and almost no chance interaction with a star goes unposted. Some celebrities choose to live heavily on social media themselves, with active accounts on which they often post about the relatively mundane and engage with fans and other celebs. How is this hyper-driven level of exposure to celebrities and the moments that exist between stages and screens affecting our relationship with them?

-

Whilst working at L'Oréal, we had the opportunity to promote a product launch into a new retailer with a meet and greet - an event hosted in-store where fans could queue to shake hands and take a photo with a celebrity as an incentive to drive footfall in-store. I'd been recently chatting with an ex-member of a popular boy band and asked him if he'd like to do it - he agreed, for a fee. The line running the length of Westfield Shepherd's Bush consisted almost entirely of groups of teenage girls, a demographic I assumed would be a little giddy, awkward and shy when meeting a star they had booked to see.

My preconception was based entirely on my own experience as a teenage fan girl when I once waited in Bluewater for three hours to meet my childhood literary hero, Jacqueline Wilson. Once I reached the front of the line, I felt so self-conscious and uncomfortable that the insightful and impressive questions I had practised in the queue completely left my body. I gawped at her like a fish on land until I was moved along by a Waterstones employee, a copy of generically autographed Tracy Beaker in hand.

Mean Girls

But that was in 2001 when the only two occasions I had seen my idol's face outside of the smiling portrait on the inside cover of her books was once in a GMTV interview and in that book signing in Bluewater. I felt connected to her work but entirely disconnected from her as a person. As I watched the tags and mentions coming in live from our Westfield event, I could see this was a very different type of fandom. I clicked through the accounts and their posts, some of which had been "liked" by the star, and saw by the pictures they were sharing that some of them had met him multiple times before. One girl's profile picture was a screenshot of when he started following her account with a date typed next to it like a memorial plaque. As they approached him in turn, there was a strange air of familiarity toward him. One group teased him about the shoes he was wearing, and another joked confidently with him as they posed for photos. One girl told him without a hint of irony that she preferred his hair when it was lighter.

What about these fans made them feel their relationship with our boyband star transcended traditional celeb/fan boundaries? The democratising nature of digital media.

-

Despite her global and seemingly immortal success, Marilyn's tragic life exposed the dark underbelly of the system that propelled her. Behind the glamorous facade, Marilyn faced personal demons and crumbled entirely under the pressures of fame. The same system that celebrated her subjected her to scrutiny, objectification, and exploitation. As Elton sang, "Hollywood created a superstar, and pain was the price you paid". She battled mental health issues and a string of very public, failed relationships, enduring the relentless pursuit of the media and an industry that prioritised her image over her well-being - "Even when you died, the press still hounded you, all the papers had to say was that Marilyn was found in the nude". On a similar but more acute thread, John Lennon met his early demise at the hands of Mark David Chapman, a fan-turned-villain who cited fame as a motive for murdering his idol.

If Marilyn Monroe were alive in the social media age, would her story have played out differently? Sadly, I think things would have somehow turned out worse. The press's role in shaping public perception and ultimately contributing to tragedy is a story we witness repeatedly, and increasingly so the more we enter a more digital civilisation. Princess Diana, the "People's Princess," faced a similar fate. Style icon, supermum, charitable and kind, she too was hounded by the relentless paparazzi and a voracious press, the public desperate to be a part of every moment of her life and the tabloids paying a pretty penny to any cockroach who could snap it. Despite her beloved public image, and largely thanks to it, it was not enough to protect her from the invasive media scrutiny that many believe ultimately contributed to her death.

In a cruel twist, Princess Diana's daughter-in-law serves as a contemporary reflection of how this situation is only becoming increasingly worse in a social media age. Meghan Markle faces relentless scrutiny and invasive media attention, media which now exists not only in print and on TV but in clickbait articles and professional and amateur digital content. Online news and social media posts serve as global town halls, with comments sections bursting with opinions and altercations. Platforms like the Daily Mail online (and other cesspits of cheap and sloppy "journalism") seem hell-bent on destroying successful and/or happy women on a mass scale. The general public seems largely to either bloody love or bloody loathe Meghan based on opinions entirely formed by media houses. Do you know her personally? I don't. Her actions have no impact on my existence, and I have no idea what her character, dreams, and opinions on Monster Munch are to form in any way a mental image of her as a whole person in order to decide whether or not I like it.

Mean Girls

Thankfully, many come to the defence of Meghan and others in her position not from liking their personalities but from an unwillingness to demonise any human being who hasn't been charged with literal crimes. In her own words, Meghan admitted to Oprah that she wanted to end her own life in response to the endless barrage of hate from the press and the public across the globe. The incessant scrutiny, fuelled by a thirst for engagement and revenue, is relentless and dehumanising. It's a system that thrives on disparaging articles about people like Meghan Markle, generating millions upon millions of ad views to sustain their bottom line.

If I ask you to picture an angry mob, you may conjure up a mental image of a marching group of disgruntled townspeople wielding mediaeval torches and pitchforks, a trope that began in 1931's Frankenstein and has been replayed in pop culture time and time again. But consider for a moment the parallels between these physical (if fictional) folks all banding together to charge against a common cause and a barrage of hate directed at a public figure online.

Let's take Frankie, a millennial person I've invented for the sake of illustration. Frankie sees themselves as a reasonably decent human being. They work hard, pay their bills on time, and occasionally check in on their elderly neighbour. One day, Frankie is scrolling on Instagram, and their thumb stops on a video of a plus-sized, scantily clad musician shaking their moneymaker. This content sparks a visceral reaction in Frankie, which could be because Frankie was raised conservatively, and they find the content vulgar. It could be because Frankie feels insecure about their own appearance, and seeing another person enjoy a freedom that Frankie won't allow themself to is upsetting. It could be a deeply ingrained societal prejudice which Frankie is unaware of. Whatever it is, it's an ugly thought that Frankie is about to reject until they notice the video's top comment. "Nothing sexy about this". Frankie feels a subtle twinge. The comment is objectively unkind but also resonates with Frankie's feelings. They tap into the comments section to read the next one, "Stop promoting obesity!". The more Frankie scrolls to read unkind and abusive comments on the video, the more validated they feel in their opinion of the content. Frankie feels connected to and accepted by the groupthink, closes the app, and continues about their day without feeling cause to reflect on how they felt about the video or the human within it.

Being inherently social beings, our ascendancy and conquest of the Earth have been fundamentally moulded by our ability to form and sustain connections. From Elizabethan England to the Victorian era, the nature and methods of human interaction showed remarkable consistency. Then, within a single generation, the digital age burst forth, reshaping how we bond and reconstructing the entire system of belonging. Our profoundly ingrained physiology, resulting from thousands of years of social evolution, is rendered useless, unprepared for a space where the complexities of online personas, distant relationships, and fleeting fandoms challenge the core of our social instincts. Can our ancient needs find solace in this new reality, or shall we remain a species perpetually seeking belonging despite all contemporary socialisation avenues? In this ever-more-connected world, are we forgetting how to connect?

-

The phrase "beauty is in the eye of the beholder" suggests that not everyone finds the same things equally beautiful. Yet, in this reality where beauty standards are at the hands of directors, editors and algorithms, and the desire to fit in is overwhelming, does this old proverb hold true? Media bosses certainly need to be held accountable for the endless ream of celebrity shaming, especially when it comes to the witch hunt for physical imperfections, but we are also responsible for how much we engage with this type of content. As I write this chapter, I find myself in the passenger seat, stuck in traffic en route to Devon caused by bank holiday travellers slowing down to insensitively gawk at an accident on the opposite side of the road. It seems that people are naturally drawn to real-life and metaphorical car crashes and emotionally invest themselves in the lives of celebrities and the culture of social media for its ugly side as much as its positive value. A never-ending conveyor belt of news and updates perpetuates this need for constant stimulation. Is this an inherent human trait or a cultural phenomenon exacerbated by the cyber machine?

The allure of celebrity misdeeds and missteps captivates our attention, drawing us deeper into a cycle of voyeurism and emotional investment. Because of how celebrities interact with social media, they feel more familiar than ever. So rare are the days when a sell-out musician or a blockbuster movie star is only ever glimpsed by paying ticket holders. Often, we can listen to music from our favourite artists whilst simultaneously scrolling through their Stories, watching them brush their cats and try on sun hats. Behind-the-scenes access to celebrities is no longer exclusive, and it's curated this insatiable sense of accessibility entitlement. Rihanna and I go way back; I joined her for breakfast this morning and even saw her family holiday snaps, so I'm entitled to know what brand of shoes she was wearing last night, right?

A good friend of mine, one of the original "beauty gurus" of the early YouTube vlogger days, took a short maternity leave when her daughter was born in 2016. As most content creators do, she had pre-filmed content during her pregnancy and scheduled it to upload while taking a break to keep her YouTube channel active. The top comment on the first scheduled video was simply, "Show us the baby."

-

One driver of this entitlement comes in the form of dopamine and its aggressive relationship with technology. Dopamine is a neurotransmitter often dubbed the "feel-good" molecule, and it functions as a messenger, transmitting signals between nerve cells, or neurons, in the brain. This chemical's impact goes beyond merely eliciting feelings of pleasure; it plays a central role in motivation, reward, reinforcement learning, and even motor control.

Every notification, 'like,' or message that pings our devices can trigger a dopamine release. This reaction is no accident; it's a calculated feature meticulously engineered by app developers and tech companies. The momentary rush of pleasure we experience upon receiving a notification or even just spotting a new piece of content encourages us to keep engaging with our devices, scrolling through news feeds, checking emails, and refreshing social media pages. The repetitive and often compulsive nature of these interactions can lead to a phenomenon known as "dopamine-driven feedback loops." As we seek out more and more notifications, our brains become accustomed to the dopamine surges, leading us to crave and rely on them for a sense of well-being. This results in overuse of technology, decreased attention span, and even addiction-like behaviours.

The instant gratification that dopamine-driven technology offers is affecting our ability to engage in long-form, focused thinking. Twitter, TikTok and Instagram Reels and Stories are tiny nuggets of news and entertainment, just a few sentences or a minute long to complete that feedback loop in increasingly shorter bursts. The patience required for deep reading, critical analysis, and contemplation doesn't satisfy our new wiring in the way that a short-form scroll hole can. Don Draper once said that happiness is "a moment before you need more happiness", and these are the bones upon which all media is built.

Social media platforms offer an enticing promise of continuous connection with others. We can effortlessly stay updated on the lives of friends, family, and even celebrities from around the world. The instant gratification of likes, comments, and shares fuels our desire for validation and social affirmation. This has also cultivated a culture where some followers expect constant updates from the creators they follow. This need for continuous stimulation has given rise to a sense of entitlement, where individuals feel they deserve access to every facet of a creator's life, from their daily routines to their most intimate thoughts. It's also sparked a nano-influencer movement, where many everyday users feel compelled to express their every thought and share their every movement with the online world.

Does this sense of entitlement to information and access to others' lives hinder our ability to empathise with and understand the complexities of real individuals offline? While social media provides a sense of belonging, it can also foster shallow engagement. Likes and comments may create a false impression of meaningful connection, masking the potential for deeper-level interactions. The pursuit of likes and followers can lead to a focus on quantity over quality, prioritising vanity metrics over genuine human understanding.

With constant posting, we also see a culture of constant comparison with others, which can lead to feelings of inadequacy and isolation. Seeing curated highlight reels of others' lives may evoke a sense of envy and the fear of missing out (FOMO). The pressure to present an idealised version of ourselves can contribute to disconnection from our authentic selves and those around us. In a future where attention spans shorten further and the sugary highs of the digital rewards system increase, might we end up in a society where nothing in the real world can compare with the virtual? Could our minds change so much that genuine experiences lose to algorithmic thrills?

-

Our subconscious mind is a little like a seagull. Whilst historically, a gull's normal survival would rely on hunting for and then managing to capture live fish, many gulls have discovered that they can satiate all hunger needs by roosting in urban environments, where they no longer need to hunt or even capture their prey, they can pull it with ease from any bin, gutter, or unwitting holiday maker's hands, any time they please. As our internet use is becoming more and more intertwined with dopamine-driven feedback loops, our brains are constantly searching for the lowest-lift, highest-reward satisfaction sources.

One Happy Hormone big hitter is the search for validation through like-minded connections. Despite the globalising nature of the digital world, where often one can feel relatively small and insignificant amongst its 5.2 billion users, many are flocking to the cosy comfort of niche communities for affirmation, empathy and a shared sense of identity.

You may think you're the only person on planet Earth who enjoys crochet, 80s heavy metal music, *and* learning about East Asian railway networks, but there is almost certainly a TikTok community, subReddit and/or Facebook group for folks just like you. You may be gay, living in a rural and bigoted physical community, therefore relying on digital subcultures to provide you with a sense of belonging and the tools to navigate life. You may hate parts of your offline life -your job, family, and responsibilities- and crafting a livelihood online provides you with validation and reason for being in a way that your *real* life can't.

Whilst niche digital communities offer these community benefits, they can also foster the arguably negative symptoms of echo chambers and tribalism. It's not always the case that these communities promote diversity of thought and open dialogue. Conspiracy theories and extremist views breed in groupthink environments, especially where those environments are used as an escape from other elements of life. Do those seeking comfort in like-minded communities risk inadvertently closing themselves off from engaging with the broader world?

Mean Girls

-

By 2018, I had already been fully immersed in, nay, raised by the Western social media status quo for over a decade. I was inside a bubble, the hazy atmosphere that normalised everything I consumed through my screens, and I was desperate to burst out and challenge my worldview. At the time, I was managing the social media channels and ambassador partnerships for a giant beauty corporation, and one of the corporate perks they offered to try and dull the sense that you were but a cog in an arguably unethical machine was a sabbatical programme. I pitched and won, and 12 weeks later, I found myself -nursing a very shit hangover the morning after my sister's wedding and ugly crying from having kissed my husband-then-boyfriend goodbye at the airport- on my own on a long-haul flight to Tokyo.

They say everything is big in Japan, and the concept of fandom is no exception. Fandom culture in the Far East tends to be highly organised and structured, with formal clubs and communities. Fans participate in collecting merchandise and attending events en masse, spanning all generations and classes. Early in my career, I did a stint covering paternity leave for the Operations Manager at a music events company in Hammersmith. My role was to organise and run the VIP packages, where superfans could pay thousands of pounds for an exclusive experience with their music icons. The thing is -and I mean no disrespect- the majority of these fans were oddballs. I always thought I'd feel the warm fuzzies watching a person get close to their heroes, but in reality, there was not a fuzzy to be felt, warm or otherwise, in seeing a middle-aged man with a not-at-all passable combover, moistly shaking hands with Adele whilst gripping an early 90s Panasonic Camcorder, especially with the knowledge that he paid three and a half grand and travelled solo from Belgium to the O2 for the privilege. One lady found out where our office was based and brought in a pie for me to 'give to Mick Hucknall'. I was convinced she'd baked her hair into it.

Click Me Baby One More Time…

In The West, it's pretty rare to come across a superfan of any individual or character unless you yourself are one. Whilst travelling through Japan and South Korea, I saw merchandise shops and vending machines on every corner and famous faces and characters on the T-shirts and tote bags of adults and children alike. While backpacking through the major cities in Japan, I often saw large groups of formally dressed businessmen and women congregating in public spaces, and it wasn't until my third week that I realised they were all playing Pokémon Go. One particularly large crowd in Seoul, made up of people of all ages, completely took over the pavement to the point that I was forced into the road to get past. My map app told me this was YG Entertainment's headquarters, a prominent record label behind some of the biggest stars in KPop.

The idol industry is deeply ingrained in the entertainment landscapes of Japan and South Korea, playing a significant role in the pop culture and media spheres in East and Southeast Asia, and with a growing presence in Western culture (Kpop has an export value of around 775 million USD). The music has a reputation for being primarily sweet, upbeat, and very -sometimes eerily- polished. Despite its vibrant facade, the world of idols is an intense and very serious business.

Idols are performers, selected and groomed by agencies from a very young age, who undergo rigorous stage and media, and sometimes modelling training during their formative years. They are raised to appeal to a young audience and, therefore, tend to look shiny and clean and require a public image. The most successful idols are banded together into supergroups, varying in talents and language ability to give them as much a global appeal as possible, and they'll often release music in multiple languages to maximise their revenue potential. Fan engagement is crucial in idol culture. Fans actively support their favourite idols through purchasing albums, attending concerts, participating in fan events, and joining official fan clubs. Fan meetings and handshake events provide opportunities for fans to interact directly with idols and establish the illusion of a personal connection.

Idols are often subject to strict image management and public scrutiny. Companies carefully control their public personas to maintain a positive and wholesome image, including rules and contracts that dictate their behaviour, dating restrictions, and guidelines for personal appearance. In 2013, a Japanese tabloid magazine published photos that showed AKB48 band member Minami Minegishi leaving the apartment of a guy from a different entertainment group, which violated AKB48's strict dating ban policy. In response to the scandal, 20-year-old Minegishi posted a tearful video on the AKB48's official YouTube channel. In the footage, she apologised profusely, expressing deep remorse for her actions and her perceived failure to abide by the group's rules. In a symbolic act of contrition, she shaved her head.

Idol careers can be relatively short-lived, particularly for members of larger groups. As idols age or seek to pursue other interests, they may choose to "graduate" from their group, often marked by a special event or final performance, and are subsequently replaced by fresh, young talent. Some idols transition into solo careers, acting or hosting, while others may retire from the entertainment industry altogether.

The world of idol culture may seem extreme to Western onlookers, but it serves as a symbolic microcosm of how businesses capitalise on our innate need for belonging. Just as idol groups are meticulously crafted to be commoditised, digital platforms and the content within them are adeptly engineered to cater to our longing for connection.

—

One of these technologies, artificial intelligence, provides a new avenue for those in the business of influencing to tap into our need for acceptance and inclusion. AI-driven tech offers unprecedented opportunities for enhancing human interactions. Imagine AI-powered algorithms connecting us not only to potential dating partners but also to friendship groups and job positions that are remarkably aligned with our unique personalities, values, and aspirations. These technologies could provide a more refined sense of belonging by enabling us to form relationships and pursue endeavours that resonate on a deeper level without all of the pain and heartbreak of pursuing incompatible matches time and time again on our own.

In this context, AI could potentially revolutionise how we approach relationships, introducing a concept where the pursuit of belonging is optimised by AI's intricate understanding of our actual preferences and needs, not just the preferences and needs we believe ourselves to have. We could rule out years of potential dating failures with the tap of a credit card and be instantly matched with the perfect life partner for us according to statistics and biometric data. While this might streamline the process of finding a life partner, it also raises complex questions about the nature of human connection. Can an algorithm genuinely understand the intricacies of human emotions and the chemistry between individuals? Would a relationship founded on AI-driven compatibility lack the depth and growth that often come from the challenges and compromises of a human connection? And is there something uniquely human and a little bit magical about rubbish dates and failed relationships?

—

AI-driven technologies today offer opportunities for enhancing human interactions. Virtual assistants, chatbots, and AI-powered algorithms tailor content to our preferences, potentially deepening our connections by providing us with information and experiences that resonate with our interests. Some of these technologies can simulate human-like conversations and companionship, offering a sense of engagement and understanding. In some instances, AI might even help bridge gaps in communication for individuals with social challenges and access ability needs, fostering a sense of belonging that might have been harder to achieve otherwise.

However, the reliance on AI for emotional support and companionship raises ethical concerns. While AI can simulate understanding, empathy, and even friendship, it lacks the depth of genuine human emotions. Relying too heavily on AI interactions could lead to a superficial replacement for authentic human connections, ultimately contributing to social isolation and emotional detachment. Whilst traditional video conferences (Teams, Zoom, etc.) are not examples of AI, they serve as an excellent contemporary example of how technology as a simulation for in-person socialisation can pose a physiological challenge for humans. In 2021, when a lot of the world was *staying at home,* Stanford researchers published a study explaining that "Zoom fatigue" -a phenomenon where constant daily video conferencing causes emotional and physical exhaustion- is largely due to the fact that it's extremely unnatural for us to spend extended periods of time making virtual eye contact with numerous people at once.

As technologies continue to advance, the challenge lies in finding a balance between using them to assist and enhance our connections and safeguarding the authenticity of human relationships. While AI might offer efficiencies and conveniences, it's essential to remain vigilant about the potential erosion of our ability to engage genuinely with one another.

-

As digital connections become increasingly intertwined with our daily lives, striking a balance between digital and offline interactions is essential to our humanity. Nurturing real-life relationships and investing in face-to-face connections is crucial for maintaining a sense of groundedness and genuine human engagement. While online communities can provide support and camaraderie, they can also exacerbate feelings of loneliness and inadequacy if not supplemented by real-life connections, and the physiological, emotional and real-life impacts of living entirely online may result in a net negative human experience.

Something's Gotta Give

.

Something's Gotta Give

Early influencers became accidentally famous. There was no industry, no brands to impress, or money to be made. People created content that made them happy about topics that they enjoyed, and the ones who were authentically the best at that attracted the larger audiences. The landscape is now unrecognisable since I entered the industry 15 years ago. We are so far away from people being able to simply post what they want, and even the most authentic creators are slaves to engagement statistics and brand pressures.

As social media continues to evolve, I've witnessed a growing bitterness among content creators and their followers. The relentless pursuit of digital popularity has given rise to a generation of creators who feel the weight of unattainable standards and the pressure to please their audiences. Likewise, followers have come to expect a certain level of obligation from these creators, perpetuating a cycle of discontent and unrealistic expectations. This industry has gained a reputation for being as cutthroat and competitive as Miranda Priestly's office. I have witnessed private feuds that disrupted campaigns and events and even more publicly known fallouts, such as the James Charles and Tati Westbrook feud, which led to James losing over 3 million subscribers within hours.

And the conflicts and controversies are not confined solely to the digital space itself. Internet superstar Zoe Sugg, widely known as Zoella, made headlines in 2021 when it was revealed that she had been dropped as a subject from a national GCSE exam board after it was discovered that her magazine reviewed sex toys. This sparked public outrage, with tabloids and their readers accusing her of attempting to sexualise her fanbase of children and labelling her as inappropriate and tone-deaf. This high-profile incident exemplifies the unrealistic and often misinformed standards imposed on social media personalities. Zoe, a 34-year-old mother of two and successful business owner, targets a demographic of millennial women through her magazine. Despite the press and public's beliefs, she has no obligation or desire to appeal to or cater to children through her work. She didn't even know she had been made a subject in a syllabus.

I know creators who have had to move house because creepy followers had managed to whittle down their addresses by studying single frames in vlogs over the course of numerous videos. One received an unaddressed, handwritten note through her letter box telling her she was a terrible mother.

-

In 2012, I was 19 years old, a second-year film student in a peplum t-shirt and hidden-wedge trainers. Rihanna was telling us all to Shine Bright Like a Diamond, wine at the corner shop was £3 a bottle (complete with typos on the label), and social media use was still primarily personal. We used Facebook to mass-upload 162 pictures taken on our digital cameras into photo albums titled "About last night" and remind each other to STOP KONY. YouTube's most-watched content was still music videos and funny cats. In some corners of YouTube, a number of people had spent the past few years uploading low-fi webcam videos from their bedrooms, inviting viewers to share in their interests such as shopping (e.g. "drugstore lipgloss haul") or fashion ("twelve different ways to wear a scarf"). These communities were slowly growing, and a small handful of YouTubers already had several million followers by this time (Felix Kjelberg's "Pewdiepie" gained 9 million followers in 2012 alone!).

Something's Gotta Give

With Gangnam Style ringing in my ears, I'd started ideating with some friends for my final major project, my Magnum Opus, a documentary about the rising industry of millennials earning a living online. The stars of this documentary were some of the most popular British YouTubers at the time, all very successful full-time creators, long before the word "influencer" had entered our vocabulary. I sat across from my course directors as we finished our pitch, and they nodded slowly. "There's a lot of YouTube in this film currently. It's interesting but very niche; we'd like to see more from the eBay sellers and the freelancing platforms. That's the future of digital earning. That's your hook". Having already spent three years working closely with creators, watching their audiences and personal brands grow, I knew these men were wrong to underestimate the potential in this industry. My stubbornness lost me the top grade for that film but has earned me a decade-long career riding the back of this soaring market. But I've encountered many a naysayer in that time - plenty of journalists, CEOs and tipsy uncles at weddings who take great pleasure in predicting The Downfall of the Influencer. This bubble hasn't burst yet, but that's not to say that there's no threat to this newer age of showbiz.

-

One way I've watched this industry evolve is with the growing impermanence of fame. A high percentage of the household names of previous decades are remembered to this day, and there's a level of immortality to the films and music of our parents' youth. The brevity of fame in the 21st century is a reflection of the fast-paced, ephemeral nature of digital media and the unprecedented volume of content being produced.

A fun (for people like me who take organised entertainment very seriously) test for this is the *birth song game*. A few websites allow you to input your date and year of birth, and it will tell you which song was number one in the music charts that week. If you were born in the '90s or any preceding decade, you'll likely be familiar with the song or, at least, the artist. It's also likely that the song represents a key moment in historical pop culture. For me, the song is I Will Always Love You by Whitney Houston and for my husband, it's Vanilla Ice's Ice Ice Baby. Despite the latter being arguably a *one-hit wonder*, I'm sure most readers know the hook, and although Whitney's song is a cover, it's one of the best-selling singles of all time.

These songs have stood the test of time because, historically, the road to fame was often paved with years of dedication, hard work, and artistic achievement. Icons of the 20th century, whether they were actors, musicians, or athletes, gained recognition through their craft and left an indelible mark on culture - their names literally pave Hollywood! The limited channels of media in the 20th century allowed for slower dissemination of information, enabling the emergence of figures whose fame was rooted in substantial achievements and resonated across generations.

If I search which song was at the top of the charts when my first son was born in 2021, the result is a song I've never heard by an artist who has only charted once more in the three years since then. He may have a cult following today, but will he still be relevant -or remembered- in ten years' time? The 21st Century has given rise to a new breed of celebrities whose fame is often built on instantaneous viral moments, reality TV stints, or social media platforms. The dynamics of the online world, with its rapid cycles of attention and constant influx of new content, have led to a more transient and fleeting form of fame. Social media influencers, who may amass millions of followers seemingly overnight, can just as quickly fade into obscurity as the digital landscape evolves and audience interests shift. Similarly, musicians propelled to stardom through platforms like TikTok may find their popularity wane as swiftly as it surged. A YouTuber or Twitch streamer could have 10 million followers without anyone outside that fan base ever hearing their name.

The sheer volume of content produced in the digital era also plays a role in the evanescence of modern fame. With millions of videos, articles, and posts uploaded daily, the struggle to stand out and capture sustained attention is daunting. While the stars of the past had a relatively limited field of competition, today's celebrities are vying for recognition in a crowded and rapidly changing digital space. This oversaturation of media can lead to a form of fame that is intense but fleeting, lacking the deep-rooted impact that defined the legendary figures of the past. It's a challenge that my talent manager friends find when choosing which creators to sign to their roster. A "good" creator (by brand and agency standards) is one with a strong relationship with their audience. With short-form content such as TikTok and Instagram Reels, is it even possible to build that connection and rapport?

The impermanence of modern fame prompts us to consider the evolution of our collective memory and the changing dynamics of cultural legacy. But the fleeting nature of stardom isn't just a result of the endless trend churn; it's also due to the fragility of cultural reputation.

-

On 31st December 2018, a Wikipedia page for "Cancel culture" was born, describing it as the phenomenon of no longer morally, financially and/or digitally supporting people—usually celebrities—or things that many have deemed unacceptable or problematic. The term has certainly taken off, sometimes having the power to dismantle somebody's career in hours, if oftentimes seemingly only temporarily.

One of the most public examples of this is perpetual YouTuber villain-turned-comeback-kid-turned-villain Logan Paul, who started his Vine channel in 2013, later migrating to YouTube, amassing a large following for what he would refer to as comedy content. In 2017, he made global news when he was publicly condemned en masse for uploading a video of a human body he found in a forest in Japan. A petition circulated with nearly 1 million signatures demanding the deletion of his YouTube channel, and the response video he released received widespread criticism for failing to deliver a sincere apology. In 2018, YouTube suspended all advertising (earning potential) on Logan's channels due to his "pattern of behaviour", referring to a joke he tweeted about the Tide Pod challenge (where children were daring each other online to eat literal detergent), removing a fish from his pond to "jokingly give it CPR", and tasering two dead rats. His revenue was temporarily halted as a result, and in response to the suspension, he broadcast live on Twitch for the first time. Two weeks later, YouTube restored ads on his channel, presumably prioritising retaining his clout on their platform over their brand's integrity and safety rating. Since then, he has continued to spark controversy with his comments about abortion and LGBTQIA+ topics, yet as of writing, his YouTube channel has 23.6 million subscribers, and he has a supposed net worth of $45M, and he seems to be continuing his high profile career relatively unscathed.

Many have criticised cancel culture as an attack on free speech and believe that it's led to extreme public censorship as creators and personalities are afraid of sparking public outrage for social faux pas and missteps. Others see it as a positive movement holding people accountable for their behaviour. I was working with high-profile personalities during the early whirlwind of cancelling and experienced from all sides the complexities of the threat of boycotting. Just like the primary school diagram of the water cycle, the ecosystem of public acceptance and rejection is complicated and self-perpetuating. Everyday folk (or, as we capitalist-bred marketers call them, consumers) have an expectation of how they imagine a celebrity to behave and a tolerance level for how much said celebrity might stray beyond that parameter. If the celebrity cocks up, then any brand aligned with that celebrity is at risk of being dragged under the same bus, as the consumer also has an expectation of how said brand should behave. Brands, therefore, tend to align themselves only with what we'd call 'safe' personalities - those least likely to cause offence, step out of line, or have a problematic past dragged up out of the digiswamp.

I've worked with creators who were metaphorically hung, drawn and quartered for a single homophobic slur they tweeted fifteen years ago when they were in secondary school. I don't know about you, but I was an asshole when I was a teenager and would hate to be held accountable now in my thirties for mistakes I made as a literal child. My inner conflict with cancel culture is that the standards we hold people to are largely very personal and nuanced. My tolerance for swearing on TV differs greatly from my grandmother's (who was deeply disturbed by Adele's repeated casual expletives in her 2016 Glastonbury appearance). However, I'm much more sensitive to misogyny than one of my male housemates in 2010s-Clapham seemed to be. Our morals and belief systems are linked closely to our sense of self, and it can feel like a personal attack on our very ideologies when we witness someone overstep these fictional boundaries.

-

The amplifying effect of digital media, the general public's predisposition to react to a headline without exploring the article, and our natural human tendency to try to "fit in" as much as possible creates a lemming effect, where one person's outrage becomes a cultural phenomenon and a personality finds themselves being cancelled by people who don't even know who they are.

That's not to say that censorship and accountability don't play an important role; it's just a very tricky balance (and one which highly paid white men in Silicon Valley are tasked with) as public standards shift and evolve. I've had marketing directors who shied away from partnering with ambassadors purely based on their proactive involvement in antiracism causes, deeming them "too risky" or "politically charged" to align with. In many cases, being Muslim or black makes you automatically too political for some directors to stomach. There's also the hell's kitchen of journalists desperately searching for the next controversial clickbait meal to feed to the starving masses. Brands have a responsibility to the people they partner with to ensure they're not sticking an apple in their mouth and popping them on the buffet table. If a brand is aligning with a digital creator and planning to propel them into the public forum through campaigning, they should already have checked that there's no bad blood for the piranhas to sniff out (because, by golly, they will). They should also ensure that the creator is aware of the risks associated with publicity, and, I think most importantly, they should be willing to stand by their decision to partner with that creator should public opinion turn sour (short of them committing an actual felony, perhaps).

-

In August 2017, I was 24, still navigating my probation period at L'Oréal, the world's most valuable cosmetics brand (worth $250bn at the time of writing). L'Oréal Paris had recently announced Munroe Bergdorf as their True Match foundation campaign ambassador, a work widely praised for its diverse representation, a still frighteningly novel concept at the time. Yet just weeks after the announcement, Munroe, who is both black and trans, tweeted, "Honestly I don't have energy to talk about the racial violence of white people any more. Yes ALL white people. Because most of y'all don't even realise or refuse to acknowledge that your existence, privilege and success as a race built on the backs, blood and death of people of colour. Your entire existence is built on racism. [sic]" This sparked a rowdy backlash on Twitter, with many users describing the statement as "racist toward white people". I switched on my work phone during my commute, and it immediately crashed, unable to cope with the dozens of thousands of notifications from the official L'Oréal Twitter account I was logged into on the device. I used my personal phone to check what was happening, and unsure what to do, I contacted my boss, who contacted their boss, who was setting up a crisis management meeting to 'address the situation.'

As is apparently customary for any globally dominating brand with a majority white leadership team, Munroe was almost immediately denounced by the group and without consulting with or notifying those responsible for talent relationships and social media channels, they released a statement on Twitter aligning themselves with the rhetoric that a certain tone of black rights activism isn't considered "championing diversity". Three years later, following the murder of George Floyd, L'Oréal joined the fanfare of brands preaching solidarity with black rights activism, and Munroe was quick to point out the hypocrisy of their behaviour. This led to Munroe's rehiring into the brand, this time not as a model but as a member of a new Diversity and Inclusion Advisory Board, a move which some would argue was less about repairing relationships with the black community and more about repairing reputation with an ever-growing consumer group whose spending power is influenced by-and-large by a brand's social responsibility acts.

-

In the age of social media, attention is currency. As individuals, brands, and public figures compete for our limited attention spans, cancel culture has become a double-edged sword. On one hand, it holds individuals accountable for their actions, challenging power imbalances and demanding justice. On the other hand, it can be weaponised, leading to the swift and sometimes disproportionate condemnation of individuals, often without due process or room offered for growth.

The control that is wielded by the social media mob has the power to raise or raze billion-dollar companies. Elon Musk, the caricature billionaire and entrepreneur, represents a fittingly almost fictional journey in the court of public opinion, from being hailed as a visionary and celebrated for his innovations in the electric vehicle industry with Tesla and his bold ventures with SpaceX to facing intense scrutiny and calls for accountability and his very public courtship with Twitter.

Elon Musk is, in many ways, the antithesis of world leaders thus far (a table at which he absolutely sits. Don't believe that politicians are the only global powers.) Some of his quirky public antics have been comically divisive - a Big Boy CEO smoking weed on a podcast? "Stars, they're just like us." To disrespectfully immature - referring to a diver involved in the rescue of the Thai soccer team from a flooded cave as a "pedo guy." To the cartoonishly villainous - a shareholder vote in 2021 to have him step down as CEO of Tesla was a response to concerns about his influence and erratic behaviour, raising questions about his suitability to lead the company. While the vote did not result in Musk's removal as CEO, it highlighted the growing unease among stakeholders regarding his actions and the potential consequences for Tesla's reputation and success.

When it comes to the scrutiny faced by Elon Musk, the calls for accountability reflect a broader societal demand for ethical leadership. One of the biggest ongoing news stories of 2022 was Musk's takeover of Twitter, which began with an indirect and seemingly satirical offer of purchase for $44 billion and ended with the mass firing of over 6,000 of the company's employees and a poll within a Tweet in which 10,000,000 users voted for him to step down as CEO (to put this into perspective, this is the size of the entire population of Sweden, Portugal or Greece). During his reign, Overlord Musk single-handedly dismantled the "verification" system, a legacy feature that had been in place for over 15 years, where notable figures were recognised by the platform with a blue tick on their profile in a bid to differentiate them from common folk and spam accounts.

Something's Gotta Give

-

The calls for accountability and consequences are rooted in the belief that individuals in positions of power should be held to a higher standard than regular folk. That those in the public eye have a moral responsibility to use their platform for good and serve as role models for their fans. In Ancient Rome, temples were the most important asset in society and culture and were built on pedestals so that they'd tower over the cities, exerting their prowess. In contemporary first-world cultures, pedestals take the form of social media followers and digital tabloid sentiment. Is it true that these people are different to you and me? Is it fair that we expect them to serve as beacons of morality and drive societal progress (and lament them for any behaviour that differs from this?)? Are we really justified in expecting them to be paragons of virtue? Some reality TV stars, such as from the globally popular British show Love Island, can catapult from a few hundred to a few million followers literally overnight. Yes, they are putting themselves in that position by signing up to be on the show, but can people who have never experienced the spotlight truly fathom its harsh glare? Until they're under it, and it's far too late to turn back.

The other argument is that burdening famous folk with unrealistic expectations stifles their authenticity. Who are we to demand flawlessness from beings who are, dare I say, in almost all ways pretty normal? As Taro Gomi says - "everyone poops"! We want to believe that the reason we spend our Tuesday mornings loading the dishwasher (again) after pulling on a threadbare pair of knickers which has been faithful to us since college, over our soft, pale ass, before commuting alongside thousands of other knackered and bored commuters, to our knackering boring jobs, whilst others spend their Tuesday mornings drinking margaritas in a Palm Springs pool with Calvin Klein models whilst staff polish silverware, is because those people are exceptional and we are not. They MUST have some otherworldly characteristic that I don't possess, which places them in their life and me in mine. And that is why they should act without flaw because they surely have none. Perhaps so, but having spent over a decade working with an array of famous folk, I can tell you that a lot of them are very ordinary people with a few privileges who happened to work hard and be in the right place at the right time.

Saying that, the Daily Mail's favourite sport is picking apart celebrities (almost always women) whose houses are *too nice* or pushchairs are *too expensive,* deeming them not relatable enough. So which is it? Aspirational or attainable? Or is relatability during stardom another impossible standard set for women in a patriarchal backdrop? Elon Musk and Logan Paul's experience with cancel culture is influenced by their identities as white men. Cancel culture often intersects with broader social dynamics and power structures, where marginalised individuals and communities face disproportionate consequences for their actions or statements. In 2001, Winona Ryder was one of Hollywood's darlings, with huge, well-loved titles under her belt like Beetlejuice, Bram Stoker's Dracula, Little Women and two Academy Award nominations. She had cameos in Friends and The Simpsons, and her career and reputation were on the up and up. In December of that year, she was detained for shoplifting $5.5K worth of goods from Saks Fifth Avenue in Beverley Hills. For the next decade, which arguably should have been her golden years, she barely worked at all, landing parts in shorts and indie films. In 2010, Darren Aronofsky cast her as Beth/The Dying Swan in Black Swan - a fallen-from-grace ex-prima ballerina with a drinking problem who winds up killed by the fresh young blood in the finalé. It wasn't until 2016 when she was finally reaccepted back into pop culture with her casting as suburban mom Joyce in Netflix's Stranger Things, a show whose vast majority of viewers are 18-29 years old and arguably too young to remember her ever being 'cancelled'.

In 2022, actor Ezra Miller was arrested on multiple counts of disorderly conduct and harassment, assault, and theft and also pleaded guilty to a burglary charge. Videos have also emerged of them physically assaulting members of the public. Despite all of this, Warner Brothers proceeded to release The Flash, a superhero movie in which Miller plays the main character, and Miller pocketed a $3M salary for the gig. Despite identifying as non-binary, Ezra Miller still benefits from privilege because they pass as a white male. We see these stories played out repeatedly in positions of status, where both men and women can fall out of favour for failures, great and small, yet often, the men bounce back, and the women fade into history.

–

Cancel culture both amplifies marginalised voices and risks silencing dissenting opinions, hindering productive dialogue. Pop culture has always been a mirror that reflects societal values and norms. In the past 15 years, social media's rapid permeation into contemporary culture has amplified pop culture's influence like never before. Celebrities, influencers, and viral trends dominate our feeds, shaping our aspirations, desires, and spending habits. While pop culture can be a powerful catalyst for change, it can also perpetuate harmful narratives and reinforce oppressive systems.

Before social media was the editor-in-chief of our worldview, there was tabloid journalism. And before Rupert Murdoch, there were public squares and players and peddlers sharing news and gossip from far-flung places. And before we were 'cancelling' people, we were blacklisting and ostracising them, and hell, literally burning them at literal stakes. In mid-late 17th Century Britain and colonial New England, we were executing women for meeting up with mates, being good at maths or having a third nipple (Harry Styles has four nipples and is yet to be set alight for it). In the 5th Century B.C. Athenians held public votes to decide who got to be cast out of society next, sort of like an Ancient Greece Big Brother. It would be remiss not to acknowledge that in European and colonial cultures historically, women were disproportionately shunned for their misdeeds - requesting rights, having babies, or heaven forbid, being single were all reason enough to be cast out by Victorian society (acts which when committed by men were met with a cigar and a jolly good pat on the back).

This disproportionate targeting of women reveals a more profound societal fear of nonconformity and the repercussions faced by those who dare to defy the norm (in this case, the patriarchy). Cancel culture, in many ways, can be seen as a reflection of this fear—a mechanism through which society enforces conformity and ostracises those who do not fit neatly into its predetermined moulds. But the impact of this need to raise pitchforks and exile en-masse anyone who offends us extends beyond historical imbalances and reaches into modern-day controversies.

Who decides what is culturally acceptable? Historically, on a macro level, it has been religion that sets the bar for most formal laws in the Global North, but on a micro level, our moral compass is set by the schools we attend, our families and peer groups, our place of work and the media we consume. Our daily interactions, including those we make online, contribute to reshaping societal norms. In the 21st Century, whilst traditional institutions still play a role, the digital age has introduced new architects of cultural acceptability, with social media algorithms emerging as powerful conduits of shaping the norm.

Social media platforms, driven by sophisticated algorithms, operate on a premise similar to the one that has historically shaped cultural norms – repeated engagement begets acceptance. In the digital realm, every click, like, share, and comment serves as a vote for certain ideas, perspectives, or narratives. The algorithms, driven by these patterns, then tailor our content feeds to reinforce the information we engage with the most.

As these algorithms dictate the information we encounter, they create a sort of echo chamber effect. Much like how religious

102

institutions or educational systems uphold particular ideologies, social media algorithms amplify the ideas that align with our existing viewpoints. Over time, these ideas gain momentum, and what starts as an individual's preference can morph into a collective ideology.

-

Toxic masculinity perpetuates a narrow and rigid set of expectations for men, rooted in the fear of appearing emasculated or weak. These expectations dictate that men must conform to traditional notions of dominance, aggression, and sexual prowess. Deviating from these societal norms can evoke a deep sense of insecurity, pushing some men towards seeking validation and belonging in spaces that amplify their fears and frustrations. How do we balance the freedom of digital expression with the need to prevent harm and maintain social order?

Enter incel (involuntarily celibate) culture—a subculture born out of loneliness and a perceived lack of romantic or sexual fulfilment. For some men, the incel community provides a sense of camaraderie, a place where their frustrations are validated and shared. Within these spaces, toxic masculinity finds fertile ground, perpetuating harmful beliefs about women, blaming them for their own perceived failures, and promoting hostility towards those who challenge their worldview.

As we explored earlier, the yearning to fit in and belong is a powerful force that influences human behaviour. In the quest to find acceptance and identity, individuals may latch onto ideologies that offer a sense of belonging, even if those ideologies are steeped in misogyny and dehumanisation. This need for belonging, coupled with toxic masculinity's fear of emasculation, creates a dangerous spiral that can lead individuals deeper into the clutches of incel culture.

Click Me Baby One More Time…

Ex-professional kick-boxer turned ex-social media personality Andrew Tate built a substantial following across various social media platforms, courting controversy and facing bans due to his inflammatory statements, often promoting violence against women. His content expresses his beliefs that women are inferior, should be confined to traditional roles, and should be treated as mere possessions. What is particularly concerning is the impact of Tate's messages on impressionable teenage boys. Teachers have voiced their worries about his potential influence, as some male students admire him and present him as an inspiring figure during class assignments.

Initially founded as a platform to combat loneliness and provide support, incel culture has evolved into a breeding ground for misogyny, objectification, and even advocacy of violence against women. While Andrew Tate has not explicitly identified as an incel, there are concerning overlaps in his ideologies and the terminology he employs. His tweets referencing the "Matrix" and the blue and red pill metaphor are embraced by incels to symbolise varying degrees of awareness and acceptance of their worldview.

Tate was charged in Romania in 2023 with rape, human trafficking and forming an organised crime group to sexually exploit women. For a decade, his controversial beliefs, inflammatory statements and provocative online persona have made him a lightning rod for criticism and backlash. While he may have garnered a following of like-minded individuals who resonate with his messages of male empowerment, his arrest stands as an ultimate rejection from society for his beliefs.

Tate's case study is an extreme one, but beyond his endless list of supervillain behaviours, the resulting discourse online serves as a worrying window into the cycle of "us vs. them," which is a tale as old as time but one which is much more aggressive and pronounced through a social media lens. Incels are created when a man feels he is being rejected and misunderstood by society. When society then rejects and misunderstands him for being an incel… do you see the pattern here? Othering leads to othering, and this is where constructive dialogue becomes increasingly challenging. Rather than engaging in thoughtful discussions, opposing camps become entrenched in their positions, leading to a cycle of hostility and division. In the case of Andrew Tate's followers, the subsequent backlash has created an environment devoid of meaningful dialogue, preventing the opportunity for genuine understanding or transformation on the part of angry, lonely men trying to protect and defend the only community they feel a connection with.

-

Conspiracy theories breed and gain strength in the same manner. For its adherents, the flat earth theory provides a sense of belonging that extends beyond just the physical shape of the planet. It's a badge of distinction, a secret knowledge that sets followers apart from the "blindly accepting" majority. Conspiracy theories function as an antidote to the mundanity or even tragedy of real life and provide means to a personal identity in a world where it is increasingly difficult to find one.

It may be easy for readers to sneer at the idea of denying the Globe's roundness, but conspiracy theories are rarely about the specific theories themselves and more symptoms of people who are often lonely, afraid, and have lost all trust in society as it currently stands. The more confusing technology makes our existence, the more people it will disenfranchise.

-

And one of the worst parts about all of this is that whilst we are all down here squabbling over who has the moral high ground and who needs to be sent to the gallows for which belief system or act, the Big Tech bosses are sitting on the top floor, rubbing their hands in glee at the sheer engagement of it all. Have you ever seen the 2001 Jerry Zucker movie Rat Race, in which a bunch of rich dudes have run out of things to do with their money, so they make up a conveyor belt of stupid sports to bet on, such as which cleaning staff can hang off the curtain pole the longest? The main race orchestrated for fun by the millionaires results in a gaggle of strangers scrambling against each other, committing crimes and causing slapstick mayhem in order to win an amount of money significant to them and disposable to the orchestrators. No matter whether we all get along or burn each other to the ground, ultimately, the social media bosses come out on top.

We may feel like we own our little corners of the internet, and the majority of my colleagues even make a living either directly or indirectly through social media platforms, but Twitter and Meta aren't gracious hosts. They are mega corporations committed to hoarding us all like I hoard plastic bags under the sink. It may feel like it's an open space because we don't pay a penny for general use, but let's not forget that we're doing the labour that evolves the platforms (and their profits).

Every action, big and small online, forms the building blocks of an elaborate data harvesting machine. This data, our preferences, sentiments, and interactions, is the modern-day gold, fueling a lucrative market of targeted advertising and consumer behaviour analysis. Have you ever heard the adage "if you're not paying for it, you're not the customer, you're the product"? This is becoming increasingly true every time we reach for our devices.

-

Every society and every micro-group within every society has a status quo and a tolerance level for those who flout it. The speed and intensity of public shaming through the digital age often leave little room for nuanced discussions or opportunities for growth and education. This can result in a toxic environment where individuals are afraid to engage in honest dialogue or express differing opinions for fear of being othered and ultimately rejected. In this sense, cancel culture can hinder the free exchange of ideas and impede progress towards understanding and transformative change.

I had a moment in my twenties where I realised that all the bullshit politics of adolescence wasn't a prelude to adulthood; it was a boot camp. A girl in my year ten class once threw an actual banana skin at me in the stairwell, an act largely in part due to my failure to be 'cool' (which was largely in part due to my failure to coat my face and lips in Dream Matte Mousse foundation each morning). In mid-2010's London, working in the corporate beauty world, I often found myself on the outside looking in. Not knowing the correct skiing terminology, not understanding high fashion and not having a Soho House membership were all reasons enough for a working-class country bumpkin not to be considered cool during most of my early career in The Big City.

-

Whilst not being accepted in your teens and twenties can be tough to deal with, I imagine navigating this life stage will be a lot more challenging for future generations as technology continues to intertwine with our reality. Rejection from society is exacerbated in a world where everything we do, say and think is recorded and broadcasted for the masses to react and respond to. Does cancel culture truly promote accountability, or is it used as a tool that enforces conformity through fear, not unlike Orwell's *1984?*

Gossip Girl

Gossip Girl

It's cliché to reference Orwell when hypothesising about dystopian futures, but one of his favourite themes to explore in his work is the controlling of society through misinformation. One of the more horrifying emergences of technology in the 21st Century has been in its shaping of the political arena, impacting not only policies but also entire power structures.

How often do you find yourself sharing news articles without thoroughly verifying their accuracy? For most of us, scrolling through social media feeds is a passive activity, and we often double-tap on the content we like without much of a second thought. By "liking" a piece of content, even if you didn't do it consciously, you are sharing it with your friends and followers, as the platform knows that people who like you are likely to like what you like. That's a lot of likes.

And whilst "likes" prove some value to the content's publisher, we often refer to these as "vanity metrics". A "like", due to the low level of commitment and thought invested in engaging in this way on social media, isn't weighted as heavily against the platform algorithm as other types of engagement and is also the least likely to indicate a consumer's intent to purchase. It's also the least accurate measure of the sentiment or popularity of a piece of content.

In contrast, "shares" and "comments" are brilliant for content publishers. If a piece of content reaches its intended audience and elicits a strong enough reaction, viewers are far more likely to share it with others and/or comment their own views on it. For content to excel in this, it must be emotive and divisive, often at the expense of being wholly accurate.

Parenting is one of the most emotional states in which a person can find themselves. It's a highly personal process, with every decision weighing heavily as you strive to not only keep a human being alive but support them in becoming a valuable and content member of society. All great parents just want the best for their children and, therefore, feel deeply passionate about their parenting decisions.

Confirmation bias is a phenomenon wherein we seek and accept information consistent with our worldview. If a parent has formed a stance on breast vs. bottle feeding, cloth vs. disposable nappies or baby-led weaning vs. purées, they will likely be defensive of this view and stirred emotionally when presented with an opposing or challenging view.

If you are a parent who exclusively formula feeds their baby, and you see a piece of content sharing support for exclusively formula feeding, you may feel inclined to double tap, to share it with another formula-feeding parent, or to comment your agreement with the post, feeling validated and assured by the content. However, if you come across a post suggesting that "breast is best, " you may feel attacked and protective of your parenting decision. You may feel inflamed by the language used in the content or the discussion in the comments section and need to weigh in with your experience to ensure you still leave the situation feeling like you made the correct parenting decision.

Now imagine that the piece of content being shared is a news article showing information about feeding babies. It may present some statistical data or some scientific research. It's likely that all you'll see when scrolling is a stock image accompanied by a headline written by a content expert with the objective of creating a reaction. The headline reads, "baby formula linked to an increase in infant mortality rates". It's an emotional subject matter whether you've got a foal in the race or not. But if you are breastfeeding your child, you may feel empowered by the headline and continue about your parenting day, affirmed by how safely you are raising your baby. If you formula feed your baby, you may feel outraged by the headline, dismissing the content as deliberately inflammatory and likely false. Either way, if you do engage with the post, you are likely to do so without actually clicking through and reading the article, your decision regarding whether you believe it or not having been made at the time you decided how you were going to feed your baby, and long before you ever scrolled onto the article in the first place.

I use this particular analogy as it's a brilliant example of confirmation bias. The data supporting formula feeding as a poor parenting decision in the Western 21st Century is very weak, but it's rare for new parents to dive into the true data to discern this; instead, almost all decisions on feeding babies come from biased and provocative articles and social media posts, often written by people in solid support of their own approach, finding data aligning with their pre-confirmed views. The echo chamber effect comes in full swing here, as most online content is not a source of information (e.g. the root data) but presents itself as such. Most pages and accounts will already have an agenda and will only link to sources (often other biased accounts) that substantiate their claims, leading to a chain of watered-down or even false data.

It's likely only prospective parents -those who have not already decided how they wish to feed their new baby- who will be searching for balanced and verifiable data, and trying to find anything neutral or impartial requires some level of skill! Not only will they be battling against millions of opinion pieces masquerading as fact, but they're also contending against an internet that thinks it already knows which side of the fence you are more likely to sit on.

Have you ever noticed that the thumbnails or cover images for films on your Netflix account look different from the thumbnails or images on your partner's? If I search for "Oscars" on my account, I'm presented with the same sea of 2022 Academy Award nominees as on my husband's account; however, for the Iñárritu film Bardo, I see an image of protagonist Silverio, smiling coyly on a train, whilst my husband sees him head in hands, looking troubled and anxious. For Tick, Tick… Boom! I see a jubilant Andrew Garfield at his piano, where my husband sees him writing, a tense expression on his face. For Heroin(e), Don't Look Up, and Two Distant Strangers, I see the films' main characters all-embracing, whilst my husband sees graphic posters devoid of human characters. We could spend an afternoon reading into what these say about the two different personalities in my marriage, but it does illustrate how the technology in our everyday lives is learning more about who we are and what we like to engage with, with every single use. Can we even trust the information we search for if the internet is motivated to show us content we already subconsciously agree with?

-

Baby feeding may have an impact on individual families but doesn't necessarily impact the total zeitgeist. But what about when fake news is used as a method to control more serious agendas?

During Pride celebrations in 2023, retail giant Target released a collection of "tuck-friendly" swimsuits designed to help conceal the wearer's genitals. The right-wing wasn't happy with the launch, and some users began sharing anti-LGBTQIA+ content (disguised as anti-Target content) on their social media channels. A few created videos claiming that Target was rolling out the collection for all ages, including children, and expressed that it would be inappropriate for children to be exposed to such a "woke" agenda as "tucking". In fact, there were no children's products produced in the tucking range, but with the virality of sensationalism, fact-checking was a lot less important than using this new information to drive homophobic and transphobic rhetoric, and soon millions of people were engaging with and sharing their own versions of the hateful content. So many people began to believe the narrative that Target's CEO needed to release a public statement confirming that the products did not exist, but by this point, of course, the damage had already been done.

It's one thing to believe a false narrative based on no concrete evidence; it's another to judge it based on evidence that is visible but isn't actually real. In March 2023, the world was taken aback by a photograph of Pope Francis stepping out in a white puffer jacket, looking not unlike a member of East 17. The image went viral across all social media platforms within a day and was convincing to even the most tech-savvy users. With many of us lacking the papal context required to discern how likely it is for him to roll around Rome in a trendy new coat, there's not enough knowledge in our minds to challenge or verify further information about the subject other than to assume it probably wouldn't happen... until we see that it would.

We haven't evolved to be able to easily identify an AI-generated image from a real-life photograph, and whilst there's nothing inherently dangerous about seeing a religious figure dressed kinda cool, what if the viral image of the Pope showed him shaking hands with Vladimir Putin, or sporting a bracelet with a swastika on it? Edgar Allen Poe once wrote a short story in which one of his characters said to another, *"The time will arrive when you will learn to judge for yourself of what is going on in the world, without trusting to the gossip of others. Believe nothing you hear, and only one half of what you see."* In early 19th century North America, Poe was very sceptical of pseudo-science and technological advancements, but a couple hundred years later, his quote is just as fitting today.

Click Me Baby One More Time…

In early 2022, stock photo company Getty Images sued a popular A.I. art company for producing artwork using stolen imagery. Software such as Midjourney and Stability A.I. trawl databases of existing photos and digital art and learn how to produce content using the information they've mined, but often pull in specific parts of that existing art to create a sort of Frankenstein's Monster of other people's intellectual property. There have been instances of artists finding their own signature emblazoned over an "A.I. Generated" image.

Other companies like Revel.ai specialise in deepfake - computer-generated video and audio content, which is currently often used to show a person's likeness when they're not really there. It's been useful for the film industry, where actors' younger selves can suddenly appear in scenes they never filmed, as in Sean Young's case for Bladerunner 2049, or where the actor has been unable to complete shooting such as after Paul Walker's death during the production of Fast & Furious 7. Deepfake in films is still a little janky and obvious but generally more digestible than weird makeup effects (looking at you, Joseph Gordon Levitt in *Looper*) or body doubles (*Point Break* is only made funnier by those plastic wigs). Metaphysic.ai run a TikTok account where they show a pretty convincing Tom Cruise dancing, working out and pouring drinks with Paris Hilton. A YouTube video with almost 10M views shows an almost imperceptively fake President Obama formally addressing the dangers of believing the content you consume online.

Ironically, the cautionary deepfake Obama video was uploaded by Buzzfeed, an example source of quasi-journalism, and one of the exact causes behind an erosion of trust in media in the 21st Century. With the proliferation of social media as the primary news discovery platform, direct engagement with publisher websites and apps is diminishing, exposing news consumers to a barrage of content that often lacks credibility.

Compounding this challenge is the presence of news sources that blur the lines between journalism and entertainment. Social media platforms host various accounts and pages that disseminate *"news"* with varying degrees of credibility. This includes accounts like *"Archbishop of Banterbury"* and platforms like Buzzfeed, which often mix news with sensationalism and clickbait. With these pages, the paradox of choice emerges as a defining feature of our media consumption. The once-clear path to reliable information has transformed into a labyrinth of options where credible news sources coexist with dubious outlets. This proliferation of sources can lead to decision paralysis, where the sheer volume of information hinders our ability to make informed choices.

Short-form content channels such as TikTok and Twitter have also become hotbeds of user-generated "news". As we consume news in bite-sized portions, a complex phenomenon undergoes a transformation into digestible fragments. However, the price of simplification can sometimes be the distortion of facts and the oversimplification of nuanced issues. In this landscape, stories are often reduced to their most attention-grabbing elements, catering to our innate desire for instant gratification.

Many traditional news publishers have recently introduced a paywall on their sites - an act that requires internet users to buy a monthly or annual subscription to the paper to access its content. Whilst, in theory, this is a critical step in ensuring the longevity of what has the potential to be a dying medium, is this also creating a divide between verifiable, restricted paid content and accessible but potentially unreliable free content? With a plethora of endless, short-form "news" available to consumers on every platform they use, are these paywalls just another barrier to entry for trusted journalism?

-

Click Me Baby One More Time...

Some instances of fake news are less obvious and far more insidious. During the COVID-19 pandemic, the East and South East Asian (ESEA) communities were struck by the sensationalism of Sinophobia spread online, mainly through trusted media outlets. In 2020, activists Viv Yau, Mai-anh Peterson, Amy Phung, Charley Wong and Karlie Wu lobbied UK government officials to call for media outlets to stop using photos of ESEA people when reporting on COVID-19. They revealed that 33% of images used to report COVID-19 in the British media in 2020 used the picture of an East Asian person in the headline, even when writing about UK towns (1.1% of British citizens are East Asian). This subconsciously enforced the false narrative that Asian citizens were carriers and perpetrators of the Coronavirus, leading to a 21% increase in anti-Asian crimes that year.

-

Do you actively seek out information that challenges your existing beliefs, or do you prefer content that aligns with your perspective? Have you ever unfollowed or muted someone online due to differing opinions? Our minds are a composite creation. They are an amalgamation of the many fragments of information we've encountered, absorbed, and internalised throughout our lives. Our thoughts and perspectives are shaped by the countless pieces of content, ideas, and opinions that have left their mark on us, from the breaking news stories we scroll through in the morning to the late-night podcasts we listen to before bed.

So, can we be confident that what we think we believe is a genuine reflection of our own minds? Are our thoughts truly our own, or have they been sculpted, refined, and sometimes distorted by the intricate interplay of digital media? Is there even such a thing as an original thought?

The democratisation of news dissemination on the Internet has disrupted the traditional gatekeeping function of established media outlets. In the past, reputable newspapers, magazines, and broadcast networks were the guardians of information, filtering and validating content before it reached the public. This curation, though imperfect and sometimes biased by political factors, often acted as a barrier against the unchecked spread of false or misleading narratives. With the advent of user-generated content and social media, this gatekeeping function has been stripped away, granting everyone the power to become their own publisher. As my grandmother-in-law recently said, "I saw on Facebook that you can't eat tomatoes these days".

This vast expanse of data that is accessible at all times may also be leading us to undervalue the depth of our ignorance and redefine what it means to trust knowledge. This growing illusion of omniscience and the dubious credibility of our sources has the potential to create a society where false or unverifiable information is the norm. Even now, I know people who will claim, "I read X piece of information the other day", only to later admit that the content they were referring to was a TikTok video.

Confessions of a Shopaholic

Confessions of a Shopaholic

The word "wanting" can describe both a lack of something and also a persistent craving for it. What is the driving force determining the things that we want? Is it a desire to assimilate with our friends or to outdo our enemies? Is it to impress our neighbours or make our parents proud? To prove our teachers wrong, or maybe ourselves? Or is it a fool's errand - a never-ending list of things we hope will make us feel fulfilled? In 2023, the luxury international estate agency Sotheby's launched a campaign with the slogan "Nothing compares to what's next". That may very well be the case if what is "next" is 300,000 square feet of Andalusian castle grounds, but when I first saw this campaign, I thought it was a parody. It's not untrue that the pursuit or anticipation of something can often eclipse the joy of the thing itself, but this tagline, to me, feels like an embodiment of the main trap of commercialism. You've finally got *the thing*. Now, what's next?

If you've bought an eyebrow product in the past decade, it's likely because of Benefit Cosmetics. In 2011, the eyebrow product market was worth £6.5M per year in the UK (around the same value as Baxter's Vegetarian Soup range, for context). Tweezer use had been rife for decades, as women did their best to show as little brow as possible (largely thanks to the patriarchal values of women doing their best to show as little facial/body hair as possible). When Burberry signed Cara Delevingne for their A/W campaign that year, she became a pop culture sensation essentially because she presented as a little more human than supermodels previously had.

Click Me Baby One More Time

Cara posted silly pictures on her social media, she told Vogue that she ate McDonald's and Pizza the day before her Victoria's Secret show debut, and she was described by those who worked with her as outspoken and tomboyish. In 2013, she proudly paraded a tattoo of a lion covering her finger. She also had prominent, unruly eyebrows.

American premium makeup brand Anastasia Beverly Hills had been growing in popularity in the early 2010s amongst the beauty gurus and millennial makeup shoppers. It was largely commercially successful because of its early adoption (and domination) of Instagram. Their brow pomade *Dip Brow* was a cult favourite product, but despite having by far the highest number of followers and engagements amongst beauty and fashion brands at the time, their product sales and commercial success didn't match.

During this time, Benefit Cosmetics, which already offered eyebrow salon services in their boutiques, noticed the popularity of Cara and *Dip Brow* and began to formulate a plan. When I joined the brand's marketing team in late 2015, I was told that Benefit's objective was to create a new cosmetics category and then own it. We made 2016 the #yearofthebrow, releasing a huge range containing products consumers had never seen before, launched a global education campaign about how "eyebrows frame the face", and spent millions of dollars on press and influencer campaigns, retail events, and disruptive experiential marketing. By the end of 2016, the eyebrow market in the UK had grown to £20M, with Benefit Cosmetics owning 60% market share, and Net-a-Porter stocked 150 different eyebrow products (up from the 20 it stocked initially). Within a few years, the average woman went from tweezing her brows thin and using no products to letting her brows grow out and incorporating brow products into the most basic makeup routines.

One of our core marketing angles was to make very clear how "unfinished" a person's face would look without the perfect, full eyebrows. There's a real art to making someone feel newly self-conscious about something they had initially felt confident in. Since the 90s, Western women were told that to be considered beautiful, amongst myriad other tasks, they needed to pluck their brows super thin and, if they were feeling *really* glam, to use a pencil to define how thin they were. Multiple generations of women were subscribed to this idea, and pop culture supported it with every model, pop star, and female love interest sporting barely-there brows and before-and-after glow-up moments such as in Princess Diaries, Ugly Betty, and most episodes of reality TV makeover shows prominently featured the taming of an originally full and natural brow.

Our team would post social media graphics of celebrities with their eyebrows photoshopped out to demonstrate how odd it made them look (I offer that the same effect could have been achieved by removing any one of a person's facial features). We adopted and promoted a "formula" for how your eyebrows *should* look based on the measurements of your face, meant as a helpful guide for customers to follow, but often received with a tinge of sadness that one's natural features were literally not measuring up to standard. I'd sometimes support on the makeup counters at the events I produced for the brand, helping to tint, wax and then make up the brows of our punters. Much more often than not, I'd be working with very sparse hairs and a very apologetic customer explaining how previous overplucking for vanity reasons had left them with nothing to work with now that thin brows were no longer beautiful. Every single employee, from the Sales Director to temporary retail staff, and everyone at HQ had targets related to the sales of brow products. Customers didn't stand a chance.

-

Influencing isn't a new concept; what's new is attaching the label of "influencer" to a specific source. Think of the enduring authority of religion on behaviour over centuries or the impact of philosophers and bards in the Middle Ages on pop culture. The advertising industry has long wielded influence over us since the advent of mass media. Even those close to us substantially shape our decision-making. So why does the term "influencers" evoke such discomfort? Is it because we don't want to acknowledge how easily we can be swayed? Does it challenge the notion that our thoughts and choices are wholly our own?

The latest evolution of the influencer landscape has emerged in recent years, with them positioned as not only the faces of consumer brands but as the brains, too. Musician Pharrell Williams' creative directorship at Louis Vuitton signals a convergence of personal influence and corporate identity and a human preference for brands to be helmed by familiar and recognisable people rather than faceless board members and senior leadership.

Fenty Beauty, the brainchild of the multi-talented Rihanna, reigns supreme here. In 2017, Robyn Rihanna Fenty took her 9 Grammys, 12 Billboard Music Awards, 13 AMAs and 7 VMAs, and her 57.3 million Instagram followers (making her one of the most followed accounts in 2017) and launched Fenty Beauty, which has an annual revenue of $582.8 million, making Rihanna the youngest self-made female billionaire.

Whilst Rihanna's success is the pinnacle of the intersection of influence and consumerism, this case is a perfect example of how having known and trusted figureheads within brands allows them to steer the zeitgeist in a meaningful way. The inclusivity and empowerment embodied by Rihanna's advertising appear much more authentic than that of a brand with a history of upholding harmful beauty standards.

This can backfire, too, however. We return to how Love Island star Molly-Mae Hague's 15 million followers across her various channels have a perceived intimacy with her due to the relatable nature of how she uses social media and, therefore, are more likely to trust her endorsements. This sense of friendship can mask the calculated strategy behind influencer-brand partnerships and the carefully orchestrated appointment of her as Pretty Little Thing's Creative Director in 2021.

At just 22 years old, with no relevant qualifications or professional experience, she took one of the most senior positions at one of the biggest fashion brands in the world, causing an internet-wide uproar. One of the main criticisms of the move was that PLT, infamous for its ethics and environmental impact, was already a beacon of the horrors of mass consumerism, and publicly appointing an influencer at the helm felt to many like a step beyond the step too far.

It would be easy to draw parallels between these business mogul creators and modern politicians. Political party leaders, often distanced from the day-to-day struggles of the average citizen by wealth and/or class, seek to represent *normal* interests to gain *normal* affections. Just as a politician may struggle to understand the intricacies and needs of ordinary lives, figures like Molly-May are often far removed from the people they're attempting to relate to, regardless of their roots. One successful fashion creator, who grew up working class but now owns multiple direct-to-consumer businesses and whom I would call a friend, recently posted a *click to shop my look* Instagram Story, which linked to a £10,000 coat.

-

Without excusing Molly-May, it's not entirely her fault that brands like PLT continue to drive our species to an early grave through the global north's obsession with consumption. Fast fashion companies like Fashion Nova, Zara and SheIn are raking in billions of dollars a year to create a seemingly insatiable need for the next new thing and then offering daily new drops to meet that need.

But what happens to those billions of dollars worth of clothes? The global wardrobe has swelled to a staggering 80 billion pieces annually, a nauseating fourfold rise in just two decades. The production of textiles contributes more to climate change than international aviation and shipping combined. And this is just the production, not considering the transportation, and then -often very soon after purchase- the disposal of the clothes.

75% of consumers recognise the importance of sustainability, with one-third saying they're willing to embrace brands championing environmental and social welfare. Often, brands will abuse this genuine desire to make "good" purchasing decisions by Greenwashing - obscuring their true environmental impact by offering "sustainable" lines as part of their mass offering. All this is, is marketing, creating another range of products to meet the needs of hungry consumers.

Often, when trying to improve the ethics of their spending, people flock to more ethical brands, and whilst it's great that there are genuine ethical brands available, all this behaviour is doing is replacing one mode of consumption with another. Many others cite low disposable income as an excuse for repeatedly shopping with fast fashion brands (versus more ethical but more expensive alternative brands). As Aja Barber said in 2022, "Most of us aren't threadbare wondering [sic] around with no shoes. We have clothes to wear". The challenge is the desire to always have something different to wear. The ever-changing trends, the fact that many of our outfits are documented on social media, and the constant pressure from ads, influencers and brands to buy the latest are all contributing to the feeling of needing to spend. Always. One contributing factor to the need for newness is that the quality of fast fashion items rarely lasts more than a few washes and becomes unwearable within a season. Another is that a rise in thrifting culture has ramped up the cyclical nature of peoples' wardrobes, with the added bonus of removing any guilt usually associated with replacing clothes in one's wardrobe.

Clothing donations and recycling points, often used to make us feel like we are *giving back* and to ease the feeling of overconsumption, are almost always not actually guilt-free at all. A significant portion of donated clothes eventually finds its way to third-world countries, filling local markets with an influx of usually low-quality second-hand Western clothing, which in turn ends up in waste piles. What may feel like charity often translates to an inadvertent disruption of local economies and the eventual littering of discarded clothes in garbage heaps. I urge anyone interested in learning more about this topic to listen to Aja Barber reading her audiobook *Consumed*.

You've probably seen people online talking about affiliate links. At its core, an affiliate link is a tracked link, usually tracking the number of times a link is clicked and the number and/or value of sales generated through that click. A brand can then attribute those results to the specific link and its poster. You could, for example, be an influencer in partnership with a makeup brand, and they provide you with an affiliate link, and each time you mention the brand, you accompany the mention with a link. Every time somebody clicks on that link to buy a product, you could earn a percentage of that sale. It's a simple and generally low-lift way for brands to incentivise creators to give them more publicity, as it's in the creator's best interest to make content that entices as many followers as possible to click the link.

This may feel hard to relate to if you don't see yourself as an "influencer", but have you ever been invited to be part of a refer-a-friend programme? You've purchased something from a brand and then receive an email that says, "If you send this link to your friends, we'll give them £10 off their first purchase, and we'll also give you money off your next purchase". That's an affiliate scheme, and brands like Hello Fresh and Estrid have become global giants by following the "refer a friend" model.

A dystopic example of this model is the online retailer Temu, which hosts third-party sellers and employs a heavy hand with its affiliate program. By converting friends to sign up to the marketplace, customers can earn vouchers to spend on its incredibly low-priced (read: 5p for a whole dress) wares, with some users claiming to be "earning" thousands of dollars by following this process. The obsession with Temu is not with the products themselves but with the gratifying process of buying lots of STUFF for very little, if any, spend. The question is, if you are paying nothing, or next to nothing, for an item of clothing, how much do you think the person who made that item was paid for producing it? What do you think is spent on their working and living conditions? What do you imagine are the quality and safety of the materials used? In 2023, an investigation was launched into Temu, which found that they posed an "extremely high risk" of breaking forced labour laws.

-

Affiliate models work so well because they are (as they are sometimes also referred to in The Biz) incentive schemes. The person sharing the link is incentivised financially to share it and encourage others to click it, and those clicking it are generally incentivised in some way by the lure of a deal or discount. By arming the average consumer to convert those around them, a brand can spread its products through the webs of society with minimal effort. My job for many years has been to find these avenues to try and drive a brand's sales through as many lowest-cost avenues as possible.

We often follow a funnel model, where the natural progression of a sale is as follows:

Person becomes aware of a product
Person becomes interested in the product
Person is primed to make a purchase
Person buys the product

A few decades ago, this process would have looked a little like this (for a fictional person called Alex):

Alex sees a TV ad for flights to Spain.

A few weeks later, someone at Alex's work gets a good deal from their travel agent on winter break flights.

After feeling for a few weeks like they'd like to get away, Alex spots a coupon for flights to Spain in their weekend newspaper and clips it out.

When they get a spare Saturday morning, Alex takes the coupon to their travel agent and books their flight.

Today, this more frequently looks something like this:

On Monday, Alex is targeted on Facebook and Instagram with ads for flights to Spain.

Throughout that same week, some of the creators Alex follows post content about their aspirational winter sun breaks; Alex is served winter holiday content on TikTok, and any website or article that Alex reads has winter holiday content advertised on banners all over the page. While browsing Facebook, Alex sees old school friends and previous colleagues Facebragging about their own trips away. On Friday, Alex receives an email from a flight comparison website with a link to deals for flights to Spain.

Alex clicks the link and is shown over a dozen airline companies and their comparative deals. Alex chooses one, is offered a PayPal pay in 3 months 0% APR price on a free cancellation policy and books their flight.

Click Me Baby One More Time

We aren't all spontaneously booking weekends away to mainland Europe, but it's a lot easier and faster to do so than ever before. This streamlining through the funnel is increased by how enabling our interactions with our screens are. The average person opens their phone 58 times per day. That's 58 opportunities to be exposed to advertising and aspiring content reminding us that our lives would be just that little bit better if we'd only spend some money. And the mechanic of spending the money has never been more straightforward, either. We can buy things immediately, with plenty of technology in place to ensure we are kept "in-app" (not switching between apps or browsers), with cookies to fill in all of our shipping details for us, and our faces confirm the payment without us needing to move a muscle. We have plenty of payment delay schemes and apps and can apply for instant credit with a single tap, making even more considered purchases much quicker to commit to. And with next-day delivery and free, instant returns, it doesn't even feel like much of a commitment at all.

By constantly chasing having the latest clothes, a shareable holiday, and an enviable home, is it the personal fulfilment we are trying to buy or the validation of others? Keeping up with the Joneses was pressure enough when the Joneses were just the couple next door - now those trying to compete and impress are doing so against billions of digital citizens.

What makes this pursuit even more complex is the nature of the content itself. Our social media profiles are often highlight reels meticulously curated to display only the most share-worthy moments of our lives. The everyday experiences can be embellished with filters and soundtracks. Holiday photos show smiles and snuggles but often fail to show the travel fatigue, bickering, wedgies or the dead rat in the pool filter. When scrolling back through our own social media channels, how much of this content can we actually relate to? Is this behaviour an attempt to erase any imperfect memories of our experiences, leaving only the good, or is it part of the show we are putting on for everyone else - the curated digital versions of us?

With many of us attempting subconsciously to measure up to an ever-expanding universe of influencers, celebrities, and acquaintances who populate our online feeds, as the boundary between private life and public display becomes increasingly porous, the inherently aspirational nature of social media can fuel feelings of isolation, anxiety, and ultimately, a sense of unattainability. While writing this section, I'm in a questionably clean bed beside my sleeping baby, listening to the rain hammering our window. Before pushing myself to open up this manuscript, I opened up Instagram. In just three scrolls, I was met with pictures of a good friend enjoying lobster rolls on a boardwalk in Maine, our best man and maid of honour clinking glasses in Lisbon sunshine, and an ex-colleague smiling on a beach in Valencia. The inadequacy, FOMO and jealousy threatened to eclipse my genuine joy for these people enjoying some well-deserved holidays, and my writing these words is a testament to my nigh-on non-existent resistance to instead switch over to Skyscanner to browse flights.

-

As is the case within a capitalist machine, supply and demand are the engine. In an attempt to escape the familiar and rarely-changing fishbowl of our own small lives, and driven by a need to consume aspirational content to remind ourselves that it is possible that we may one day spring out to enjoy the pleasures on the other side of the glass, we really prefer to view the new. One of the most popular social media trends since the birth of the industry is the "haul" - a practice in which somebody will buy a bunch of things and then share what they've bought with the internet. In the early days of digital beauty and fashion content, this was the leading style of video or blog post, and this has now extended across every consumer category imaginable (the top ten most popular "haul" videos on YouTube currently have a combined viewership of 321 million).

A sibling to "haul" content is unboxing, wherein a person unwraps something they have just bought on camera. These videos, like hauls, are so popular because they trick the viewer's brain into feeling like they themselves have just bought something new. The cheap, easy, instant gratification that comes with watching another person buy and open up a product alters the chemicals in the viewer's brain, releasing dopamine and delivering the satisfaction of buying without the actual spending. The top ten most popular unboxing videos have a combined viewership of 585 million and are largely comprised of luxury products like sports cars, designer bags and high-end tech gadgets, allowing viewers to experience what it would feel like to purchase something many of them will never actually get the chance to. One more disturbing subcategory of this type of content is children's toys.

The Google-owned platform Think With Google, which offers advice and data for marketers wanting to reach customers through Google products, published a helpsheet in 2014 called *The Magic Behind Unboxing on YouTube,* telling video creators how to leverage "giddy, child-like anticipation" and the "emotional feeling that unboxing videos elicit". There are now hundreds of millions of videos on the internet that feature a person (almost always an adult man) unwrapping and playing with children's toys. Once, whilst sitting on the runway for the second hour of our delayed flight with a very bored and upset one-year-old, I opened up YouTube Kids on my phone and clicked on the first video on the homepage. It was a video of a man's hands going through a pile of Hot Wheels boxes, opening them one by one and then "driving" them off the screen. The trance it put my son in was immediate and alarming, and although it quietened him, his physiology so closely resembled someone who had taken class-A drugs that I felt certain the content was literally destroying his brain cells.

We watch screens most days as a family, and I do not judge any parent who uses them for any reason. Still, I find the effect these sorts of videos have on my children unsettling, and we choose to stick to slower, more narrative-driven content that we can discuss together as a family - some favourites include Postman Pat, Bluey, The Adventures of Paddington and my boys' godmother Miss Rachel.

The fact that Google created this helpsheet shows that the demand from viewers for this kind of content has been high for some time. The Google Trends tool shows that the search terms "haul" and "unboxing" have remained pretty constant globally over the past decade, almost always peaking in the summer months and waning in the winter. This drop is likely because December is when many people give and receive gifts and are therefore experiencing "unboxing" gratification IRL. Content creators reflect our society's collective desires, and people are often quick to demonise them without understanding the gravity of how much our search queries shape the content landscape. In 2019, the top earner on YouTube was an 8-year-old boy.

Oh, Baby, Baby.

Oh, Baby, Baby.

Born during and after the early 2010s, Generation (Gen) Alpha is the first generation to have grown up in an entirely digital society. My two boys are Gen Alpha, and I often find myself awake at night wondering what their relationship with technology will be as they come of age and what I can do to encourage healthy, safe, and savvy digital lives.

Throughout my career, this topic has been very prominent. I'm regularly asked to discuss children online in the press, on stage, and in podcasts, and I am often cornered at BBQs and weddings by parents who learn what my field of expertise is and want advice on setting their children up with social media accounts. When I ran my agency, some of the most common proposals we would receive would either be from brands wanting us to create campaigns to reach children online or from "family" influencers looking for brands to sponsor their channels.

In 1935, Shirley Temple was given an Academy Award at just five years old. She was earning $2,500 per week in her contract with Fox (equivalent to $56,000 today) with a bonus of 6x that for each finished film. She was contracted to shoot at least four feature films per year and was involved in colossal licensing and advertising deals, from dolls to cigars. Young Shirley starred in over 40 films in total and was subject to almost every nightmare Hollywood has to offer, from on-set abuse to vicious tabloid rumours. It's been widely reported that Judy Garland, whilst on the Wizard of Oz (1939) set at sixteen years old, was forced to survive on a diet of black coffee and 80 cigarettes a day to keep her thin and alert during long filming days.

It's been long accepted that child stars rarely make it to adulthood intact. When I was at university, my friend took me to a gig for a small band called The Pizza Underground, a rock group who sang covers of Velvet Underground songs but changed the words so that they were about pizza instead. The frontman was 90s cinema darling Macaulay Culkin.

The public and press of recent decades have loved following the lives of famous kids who eventually "go off the rails". The hounding of Hollywood's past sweethearts -Miley Cyrus, Britney Spears, Gary Coleman- and deplorable glee when their lives fall apart is unsurprising and dystopic. I once ran a campaign with a celebrity who had starred alongside Lindsay Lohan in the mid-2000s, who told me that she was the most fragile and exploited person he had ever worked with. In 2022, actor and writer Jeanette McCurdy published a best-selling autobiography exposing the pressure, abuse, and exploitation she faced during her childhood as a Disney Channel employee.

The D'Amelio sisters, Dixie and Charli, rose to the top of TikTok as teenagers and are now multimillionaires, earning hundreds of thousands of dollars for every brand deal. Snapchat reportedly paid them $100,000 each per 8-minute episode of their *silly challenge* series, and in 2021, streaming giant Hulu commissioned them for a reality TV show about their family life. In one episode of this programme, we see 16-year-old Charli sitting in a room with her family and a team of agents and publishers, planning out her year ahead much like senior marketing teams do for consumer brands. They list off starting a clothing company, books, TV shows, and "as many business ventures we can start at once". A nervous Charli responds, "This is definitely a lot more stuff than I thought I was doing".

Oh, Baby, Baby.

The D'Amelio family, who moved from a New England suburb to a mansion in LA, now live a luxury lifestyle financed almost entirely by their youngest child. What are the implications to a child when their parents are financially dependent on them? In an era where many young people find fame for things that wouldn't necessarily be considered a talent, they need to learn monetisable skills retroactively to remain lucrative.

-

I've worked with thousands of adult creators throughout my career and have met very few who have never experienced the negative side effects of a life and career so public online. In 2021, the New York Times ran a feature describing the stress and burnout of being a content creator titled "Young Creators Are Burning Out and Breaking Down". It's common for creators to suffer from panic attacks and anxiety, turn down work or pause their accounts due to mental strain, and suffer the toll of trolling, abuse and high expectations at the hands of followers. The constant pressure to evolve, adapt, and remain relevant but authentic has caused many early influencers to step away from the industry altogether.

It alarms me then whenever I see a child starring in or hosting content on social media. Not only would a child be less equipped to cope with pressure, trolling, and anxiety than an adult, but they also lack the maturity and experience even to comprehend what it is they're signing up for and the potential toll it will take on their well-being.

Loann Kaji is the mother of Ryan, the little boy who is the face and star of a multimillion-dollar enterprise that began as his YouTube channel, Ryan's World. In an interview in 2019, when Ryan had already made an estimated $59 million at eight years old, Loann claimed that recording the videos was an opportunity for the family to "spend time together" and that "Ryan loves recording videos". She's also adamant that Ryan's content is a good influence, with partnerships like Colgate toothpaste encouraging good behaviour and habits in Ryan's young following.

Many argue that there is something deeply exploitative about putting a child in the spotlight and then monetising the result. Whilst it may be true that creating content is an enjoyable hobby for many and that some of this money will be used to create opportunity and security for the child's future, can these potential positives outweigh the risks of a life online, and more importantly, should a child be allowed to make that decision for themselves?

Not every child's experience of digital fame comes in the form of a considered and managed channel. Every day since the social media boom, a new video goes viral featuring a child doing something funny, cute, clever or "naughty". The most viewed video in the early days of YouTube was "Charlie Bit My Finger", a 56-second clip featuring a 3-year-old and his 1-year-old brother, which has been viewed in multiple forms nearly 1 billion times. It was sold as an NFT for $761,000 in May 2021.

Each time you open your phone, it doesn't take long for you to be served with content of a child who was filmed and published on the internet without their consent. Often, this is done by a parent hoping to *go viral,* to taste their tiny moment of fame by using their child as the hook in the content. Sometimes, it is the case that parents piggyback on social media trends - the one that is circulating the week that I draft this section is the *egg crack* trend, where adults set up a camera with an unwitting child in the shot and then surprise them by cracking an egg on their head. This trend and trends like it are pretty upsetting to watch, as you see the confusion, distrust and pain in the little one's face, met with the laughter of the grown-up who has already decided they're going to share this footage on the internet. As with any trend, the comments sections are constantly divided, with many calling this "light-hearted banter" and arguing that kids will grow up "too soft" if

Oh, Baby, Baby.

their parents don't expose them to experiences like this. I've yet to find a scientific data source that supports publicly humiliating a child as a method of building character.

There's also the case of adults who become parents after already building a fan base and digital platform. When looking at the higher tier of celebrity, such as the Kardashians or the Beckhams, we can see many examples of families where the children have almost as much star power as their parents. This filters down into the realms of social media celebrities, who have been criticised for accessorising their content with their children, introducing them as new characters into the brand of their channels. This is especially true of creators who post vlog content, many of whom don't shy away from giving their children starring roles in their videos. When you share every facet of your life with the internet for your job, and your children are some of the most important elements of your life, I can definitely see how this ends up happening.

I have many creator friends who have chosen to almost completely omit their children from their content, almost as if they don't exist. This is also met with criticism as they're labelled as cold or disinterested in their own children, despite the fact that a person's social media content is just a tiny, curated snapshot of their reality. The majority of creators close to me tend to reference their children and parenthood but only when relevant and cover their children's identities at all times.

I have taken over 50,000 photos since my first son was born, and I can confidently assume that at least 44,000 of them are of my kids. I'm immensely proud of everything they do and am sometimes desperate to share them with the world. Until my eldest turned one, I would post pictures and videos of him smiling, dancing, walking, and eating with all the enthusiasm and wild abandon of Peter Rabbit in Mr McGregor's garden. Still, as he's gotten older and since his brother joined our family, this need to always share my children has been replaced by a need to protect them.

143

Click Me Baby One More Time…

Those who grew up in the 80s and 90s will be familiar with the concept of *Stranger Danger,* a campaign reminding children of the risks of interacting with unfamiliar adults. Most schools had a rumour that there was a van roaming the neighbourhood, its driver bundling unsuspecting kids into the back, and standard parental advice when leaving the house was, "Don't talk to anyone you don't know!". This call for heightened fear of strangers has quietened over the years, as data shows that less than 1% of missing children are abducted by strangers, and over 90% of child sexual abuse cases are committed by people known or related to the child.

In the digital world, however, the risks posed by strangers are much more rife and still much less discussed or policed. The information we share at any given moment, such as what the outside of our homes looks like, what colour our children's school uniforms are, or tagging our location, can all be used by ill-intended people for ill-intended purposes. In the physical world, such as when I take my boys to the park, I can watch for risks. I can spot a stranger hiding in a bush or sneakily attempting to take photographs, and I can keep my boys within eyesight and arms' reach at all times (despite their every intention to run in opposite directions at any opportunity).

Online, although we don't like to think about it, our children and images of them are unattended, and strangers aren't hiding in bushes; they're active, undetected internet users. Instagram's Sticker feature called "Add Yours" encourages users to join a gallery of other public users in a chain of topics such as "Add Yours: Your silliest pet photos" or "Add Yours: Your baby then vs. now". These can be cute to join in with and tickle our FOMO pickle, but how many users are clicking through to see who created the trend? In fact, Instagram offers an anonymity feature, where the person creating the Sticker can hide their identity. How many

144

Oh, Baby, Baby.

people who add their personal photos to the gallery stop to consider whether any user could access this collection of images?

And what about the ways in which the information we upload can be used for real-world crimes? A new type of burglary to rise in the past decade occurs because the homeowner has posted about being on holiday, advertising to robbers that their home is left vacant. With the amount of information the average internet user posts about the identity of their home, even without realising it, it's not surprising that professional criminals are targeting their victims based on social media posts. At the age when my children stopped looking like generic babies and also started spending time away from me (when starting childcare), I stopped sharing their faces online. If a stranger were to approach one of my children when I'm not around because they recognised their face, and this stranger knew my name, my children's names, and other details such as my work or places we had recently visited, my children and any caregiver with them would be disarmed by this familiarity, leaving them vulnerable.

-

Another reason why I and many others are reluctant to post our kids' faces on social media platforms is one of data. As we've explored throughout this book, every single interaction we have with our screens provides some data to some collector. Our likeness -the representation of our physical image- is data, and the digital platforms we interact with use that data to create profiles and understand user preferences, behaviours and interests. They use our likeness to tailor advertisements and content recommendations. The terms and conditions, which none of us read but all of us accept, involve us relinquishing a certain degree of ownership and control over the data we share. Season 6 of Charlie Brooker's Black Mirror opens with the episode Joan is Awful, in which a woman's life is ruined by a streaming service's portrayal of her life on screen. When Joan attempts to sue the

145

company for using her as a character for the show against her knowledge, she is presented with the Ts and Cs contract she ignorantly signed when registering to be a customer of the streaming service, granting them irrevocable rights to do whatever they want with user data.

The growing integration of facial recognition technology into apps and social media platforms raises significant concerns regarding user privacy and data ownership. While users may be familiar with providing this data for high-security purposes, such as bank or passport verification, the other current and potential uses of this data are not publicised or explicitly stated. In the context of Europe's General Data Protection Regulation (GDPR), which emphasises the importance of user consent and data transparency, Meta's practices come under scrutiny. The GDPR emphasises *meaningful* consent, ensuring that users are fully aware of what data is being collected by a company and how they intend to use it. However, companies like Meta bury content clauses deep within lengthy, jargon-y terms of service agreements, leaving users with little clarity.

And whilst most users consent to these terms regarding their own faces and likeness, they also make the same consents on behalf of their children. A child's face is recognisable by algorithms from birth. A test of this is to find any image of your child in your iPhone Photos, swipe up on it, and click the bubble in the bottom left-hand corner of the image. In doing so, you'll be presented with a stream of photos of your child at all ages, correctly identified by the phone as being of the same person. This is the same technology that Facebook used a decade ago to tag friends in your group photos without their knowledge, and some physical shops use it today to identify known shoplifters and track frequent customers. We don't currently know what tech companies will do with this technology and data in the future, but we do need to consider if we've already signed the consent form for our children's faces to be used, will

Oh, Baby, Baby.

these rights be revocable in their future, or become indelible markers of a digital footprint they didn't choose for themselves.

-

While my not-yet-two-year-old was eating breakfast in his high chair, I left the (silent) room briefly to let the dog out for a wee. I reentered the room to "early in the morning, just as day is dawning, he picks up all the post bags in his van". I waved towards our Google hub to pause it, thinking I must have accidentally pressed play on the song in my pocket, yet as I started to boil the kettle, I heard a little voice behind me ask, "Hey Google, Postman Pat, Spotify".

My sons will turn 18 in 2039 and 2041. Researchers suggest that they will spend, on average, 4.5 hours per day of their childhood looking at screens. With studies showing that every hour spent on social media increases the likelihood of feeling socially isolated by 13%, and with all of the topics we've explored in these chapters, I'd be forgiven for fleeing with my family to the Tibetan mountains and abstaining from technology for eternity. But I'm not going to do that, and neither are you, so let's explore this further.

-

Not only will our children be the first generation to grow up entirely in a digital age, but they will also be the first *consumers* to do so. As overwhelming as it can feel, it's just as vital that we learn and understand the apps and devices our kids have access to as it is that we know how to keep them safe in the car or at home.

Chat rooms and forums have long been recognised as some of the more dangerous corners of the web. The spaces can foster genuine relationships and allow people to forge connections with like-minded folk, but they are also often notoriously unmonitored and allow users to remain anonymous or, worse, use false identities when communicating with each other. Many apps and games - including those that children use- have chat room functions. Roblox and Minecraft are two of the most popular online spaces for children, with 350,000,000 monthly active users across both platforms. 56% of Roblox players are under 12 years old.

Within both of these games, there are chat boxes and voice chat functions, and whilst these are age-restricted and heavily monitored, there have been countless cases of children engaging in inappropriate conversations with each other and adults posing as children within the games.

As children get older and gain access to their own smart devices, which they may sometimes use without parental monitoring, other apps not designed with children in mind pose more threats to young, impressionable minds. There are forums and social media channels that promote eating disorders, offering advice and encouragement to viewers to not only adopt unhealthy eating habits but also how to conceal them. Porn, violence and other inappropriate content exist in plain sight on easily accessible channels, and you may never see those sorts of videos because they're irrelevant to your online profile, but that doesn't mean they're difficult to find.

When I was a teenager, the Bluetooth function had just become available on some phones, and for the first time, we could share video content from one device to another almost instantly. The sexually graphic video titled Two Girls, One Cup was shared with and viewed by almost every school child with access to a mobile phone in the mid-2000s, but besides this, the majority of the content we were consuming at the time was benign and relatively age-appropriate, if not for a little foul language.

Oh, Baby, Baby.

Aside from the threats to safety, there are other ways in which these platforms, if we don't correctly understand, monitor and educate on them, can generate risk for our families. The average Roblox user spends $60 per year on in-game purchases, although there are plenty of examples of children spending more than this, such as the ten-year-old girl in Denbighshire, UK, who changed her family iPad password to spend £2K on the game, or the Floridian 7-year-old who wiped his mum's bank account buying Robux, the in-game currency. A recent news story emerged of a 13-year-old girl in China who spent $64,000 over four months on mobile gaming.

The thing is, just like all other consumer-facing brands, these games and apps are engineered to be addictive. Entire teams are working within these companies whose job it is to encourage users to spend their money within the app and to incentivise them to want to play more.

Because children are especially impressionable, and because it's becoming increasingly easy for minors to make purchases without parental consent through digital devices, there are bans in place in many countries to prevent the advertising of particular products, like junk food, to minors. In 2019, YouTube and its parent company, Google, had to pay a $170 million fine for violating the Children's Online Privacy Protection Act (COPPA) law. The accusation was that YouTube illegally collected the personal data of individuals under 13 years old to create targeted advertising on the platform. As a result, YouTube was obligated to introduce a new policy specifically for content aimed at children, under which videos created for children are not allowed to be monetised, and comment sections are turned off.

I was once at a breakfast event hosted by the UK's Advertising Standards Authority (ASA), which featured a panel of top marketers discussing the changing advertising landscape. A representative from one of the biggest confectionery companies in the world was present, and he asked the panel, "With the new restrictions in place, how can I use influencer marketing to reach our core market for our kids' products?". He was advised that in order to work around the guidelines, he should partner with content creator families on their content not flagged as "for kids".

A person's mother tongue can significantly influence their approach to maths, as linguistic and cultural nuances shape our thinking patterns. For instance, languages with irregular number words, like English's *eleven* and *thirty-one*, require an increased cognitive effort for basic calculations. This is compared to a transparent number system like in Cantonese, where 11 would be referred to as *ten one*, and 31 would be referred to as *three ten one*, making it clear that 31 comprises three units of ten and one unit of one. Whilst to a native English speaker, this may not look like it would make much of a difference, the cognitive effort required to solve equations in a transparent number system is dramatically reduced, and children who grow up speaking these languages are faster and more accurate at mental arithmetic.

This phenomenon is an example of neuroplasticity, the way in which the brain reorganises itself by forming new neural connections in response to learning, experience and environmental changes. With Gen Alpha growing up in an all-encompassing digital world, how will their brains shape and mould along with their environments? The digital sphere fosters rapid information absorption, which could lead to reduced patience and attention spans. With algorithms and brands informed by big data predicting desires before they're even articulated, might Gen Alpha develop a reliance on technology to understand their own needs and wants? An over-reliance on predictive technology could lead to a society that looks externally for answers, even to deeply personal questions. Critical thinking abilities could be reduced due to how information is curated online. As the platforms we use continue to strive to deliver comfort through familiarity, what happens to our intrinsic desire for exploration and curiosity?

My husband, an accomplished engineer, has been developing software since he was 14 years old. In our household, digital literacy is as essential as learning phonics and colours. The risks and dangers posed by giving our children access to technology can feel overwhelming and frightening, but we see it as our responsibility as parents to stay informed about evolving technologies and their potential impact on our family, as well as to educate our kids on digital citizenship, media literacy and safety as much as we teach them to cross a road safely. Technology is a certainty in our kids' lives, so we want to guide them through their access with boundaries and parameters that protect them as they explore and discover.

-

Our children will be shaping the future digital landscape just as much as the generations before them. Whether you like it or not, it's not just blue-ticked celebrities and multibillion-dollar corporations who impact the online world. Through our swipes and taps, we influence each other and the platforms we interact with daily. Influence isn't a one-way street; it's more of an intersection with a continuous, chaotic flow of traffic. You might follow someone for their fashion sense or their pasta recipes, yet unknowingly absorb their political leanings or even their lexicon. Some of your greatest lifetime memories could be formed on a holiday you booked because you saw a creator's #ad about the hotel. Influence is subtle; it's the subtext that sneaks in whilst you're busy engaging on the surface - as we are creating our digital environments, they are creating us, too.

While the dangers and risks of a generation born of modern technology are very real, so are the opportunities for creativity, connection, and progress. By fostering digital literacy, critical thinking, self-esteem and a strong sense of ethics, we can guide future generations to thrive in a digital age. Like with alcohol, social encounters, traffic and grapes, it won't always be possible to shield our children from every danger in life. We can, however, equip them with the tools and knowledge to make informed decisions and cope with consequences as they experience the world in their own way. One day soon, we'll be passing the virtual baton to them, and as we are withering away in our hover-chairs, they'll be guiding the next generation safely through the digital landscape, building a world that reflects the best of our shared human potential.

Acknowledgements

I've been putting off writing this section because I know that I'm both going to forget someone important and offend them horribly, but also not do justice at all to those I do remember. I also find these sections to sometimes be a little self-satisfying so I'm going to attempt this in a chronological order.

I struggled a lot in school - all I wanted to do was read fiction, write down my thoughts, and chat and that didn't lend itself well to the majority of my state school classes. Unsurprisingly it was the librarians and English teachers who found me the least irritating, and Saira Sawtell in particular was always so encouraging. I thought of her lots when I wrote this book (especially when paragraphing!)

During my TV and film degree the modules I enjoyed the most were the theory ones. I cared less about the two-point lighting setup or how to create a DVD menu (one of these proved to be more useful to my career than the other), and much more about how the introduction of on-demand-video would revolutionise the type of programming that would become popular in the future. Two professors who revelled in my need to nerd out were Karen Randell and Stuart Joy. I'm forever grateful for their support and infectious passion.

The first person to teach me the ropes and introduce me to the people who powered my career in the beginnings of the industry was Patricia and I owe so much of those early years to her. She was extremely generous with her time, connections and money for the years I worked with her.

Click Me Baby One More Time…

The past 8 years of my career have been filled with some incredible women who took a lot of chances on this common bumpkin and taught me most of what I know today. A special thanks to Annie Harrison, Kyra White, Hayley Roughton, Fi Halstead, Luciana Andreoni Clayton, Rema Fromant, Camilla Craven, Manuela Cripps, Hannah Regan, Soph Blackhurst, Viv Yau, Maddie Barsch, Bronagh Monahan, Sophie Gildersleeve, Charlotte Stavrou, Katie Cottam, Caroline Finn, Alice Audley whom have all given me incredible opportunities and special companionship over the last decade in various roles.

I'm also incredibly grateful to all of the Creators whom I get to call colleagues and friends. Some who have been on the other end of a voice note or WhatsApp message for many years include Sam Maria, Victoria Magrath, Robyn Donaldson, Ben Heath, Lily Pebbles, Zoe London, Paige Joanna, Ben Pechey, Ellie Middleton, Josh Cuthbert, Amy Bell, Anna Newton, Megan Ellaby, Shannon Robinson, Carly Rowena, Beth Sandland, Fleur Bell, Manal Abdul, Linda Sanchez and so many more. To work with so many examples of the beauty of this industry is a privilege and an honour.

I also owe a lot to the person most people in my field of work call the Founding Father of the Influencer Industry, Dom Smales. He built the world which introduced most Creator Economy practitioners to the concept of this being a job. In recent years he's always on the end of the phone for a sense check, and seems to never run out of opportunities to introduce me to powerful people.

One of those people was Rikhi Ubhi from Bonnier who believed in me from the beginning and helped create so much structure and order to this book.

Thank you to Ruth Crilly who agreed to be the first to read my

156

Acknowledgements

manuscript despite being knee deep in her own book launch (please buy *How not to be a Supermodel*).

Thank you to the staff in my local Costa who entertained my almost daily presence for four months, whilst I stole your ambience for nap times so I could find snippets in which to produce the bulk of this work. One of them once referred to me as "The Writer" and I had a happy cry about that.

Thank you to my mum in advance for definitely being the only person who will buy multiple copies of this book. She taught me that good things come to people who work hard and stay kind, and that people like us are still allowed to dream big.

I'm so sorry to anyone who doesn't have a husband like mine. We met at uni in 2012 and fell properly in love and promised right at the start to always support each other in the pursuit of success. He's sacrificed a tremendous amount for me to chase my dreams. He's my harshest critic and my biggest cheerleader. He makes the best teas and even better babies. I fancy the pants off you, B, and you inspire me beyond words.

And to my boys, Mars and Sage. When I'd finished writing my book we took a 7 month summer together to play trains and watch movies and have picnics and read books and it's the best decision I've ever made. Watching you grow is my life's greatest joy.

My Recommendations

Reading

Emily Oster' books are a data-driven dive into some of parenting's most challenging decisions.

Philippa Perry's books will force you to have a cold hard look at the way you conduct relationships and the reason behind your love and friendship challenges.

Yuval Noah Harari's *21 Lessons for the 21st Century* and *Homo Deus* are academic works of art, exploring all of the fears we have about tech in the future.

Simeon Brown's *Get Rich or Lie Trying* contains some incredible real-life character studies from within the world of Social Media.

My Recommendations

Listening

The Rest is Entertainment is a wonderfully informative and light podcast which lifts the curtain on the media industry.

The Influencer Marketing Lab podcast interviews some of the most influential puppeteers of the creator economy.

Aja Barber's *Consumed* tells you everything you need to know about your role as a person who shops in the 21st Century. I much prefer the audiobook as it allows you to explore the book in Aja's voice.

Watching

Black Mirror is a really troubling and important series with almost every episode asking the question "how is technology endangering our lives?" and "how far would you go to protect what is most important to you?". My favourite episodes are *Hang the DJ, The Entire History of You, Fifteen Million Merits* and *Men Against Fire.*

The Social Dilemma and *The Great Hack* are two documentaries which I recommend to people who don't work in my world. They shed light on important moments in technology history which impact us all.

Zeynep Tufekci's TED talk *We're building a dystopia just to make people click on ads* is a brilliant watch to dive into some of the topic we've discussed here on a deeper scale.

About the author

Geo has been named one of the biggest influences on the Influencer Industry. She began her career working with YouTubers and Bloggers from her student bedroom in 2018 and has been a vital part of the influencer industry as it has grown into the $21 billion giant it is today. Since then, Geo has led campaigns for global brands such as L'Oreal and EA Games, founded and run an award-winning influencer marketing agency, and worked with the biggest celebrity names on and off social media, from your sporting hero, to your Hollywood crush, to your daughter's favourite YouTuber. She is a guest writer and public speaker, leads digital marketing training courses and was awarded the highest-rated influencer marketing educator in 2022. Geo also sits on the advisory board for numerous industry award bodies. She is an honorary judge for the Influencer Marketing Show and bCreator 2023/24. This is her debut book.